To Bob,

D1046127

Yes We Did

AN INSIDE LOOK AT HOW SOCIAL MEDIA BUILT THE OBAMA BRAND

RHarfoush

BY

Rahaf Harfoush

New
Riders

VOICES THAT MATTER™

Yes We Did

AN INSIDE LOOK AT HOW SOCIAL MEDIA BUILT THE OBAMA BRAND

Rahaf Harfoush

NEW RIDERS

1249 EIGHTH STREET ❦ BERKELEY, CA 94710
Ph (510) 524-2178 ❦ Fax (510) 524-2221

FIND US ON THE WEB AT:
WWW.NEWRIDERS.COM

TO REPORT ERRORS, PLEASE SEND A NOTE TO:
ERRATA@PEACHPIT.COM

NEW RIDERS IS AN IMPRINT OF PEACHPIT, A DIVISION OF PEARSON EDUCATION

PROJECT EDITOR	¶	MICHAEL NOLAN
DEVELOPMENT EDITOR	¶	MARGARET ANDERSON
PRODUCTION EDITOR	¶	TRACEY CROOM
COPY EDITOR	¶	GRETCHEN DYKSTRA
PROOFREADER	¶	ROSE WEISBURD
INDEXER	¶	VALERIE PERRY
DESIGNER	¶	SIMPLESCOTT
PHOTOGRAPHER	¶	JESSE MORGAN

ISBN-13: 978-0-321-63153-4
ISBN-10:   0-321-63153-6

9 8 7 6 5 4 3 2 1

Printed and bound in the United States of America

DEDICATION

*To Nabil, Hanan, Rania,
Riwa and Jesse*

SPECIAL THANKS:

To Chris Hughes, for being so generous with his time and expertise during this campaign. To the Chi-New Media Team, I will always treasure our memories, friendships and good times together. To my Godparents, Jan and Trilly for offering me a safe haven during my writer's block. To Scott Thomas for his beautiful work in designing the cover and book layout. To my mentor, Don Tapscott for his wisdom and encouragement. To my tribe: Michael Dila, Robin Uchida & Mary Jane Braide without whom I would have never embarked on this journey. To Pigeon for her mastery of all things Google. To Eva Szymanski for her uplifting pep talks during difficult chapters.

To the New Riders team for their support during this process, especially Michael Nolan and Margaret Anderson.

Table of Contents

FOREWORD

The Obama Experience:
Redefining Elections, Democracy, and How to Get Things Done in the Digital Age

Yes, the "improbable victory" of Barack Obama redefined elections. The body politic in the United States will never be the same. But as the president attempts to lead the rebuilding of our devastated economy, failing ecosystem, and deeply troubled world, it's no exaggeration to say that he is also redefining how we govern and the nature of democracy itself. The experience is rich with lessons for every government, business, and organization.

The Internet and an extraordinary social movement enabled him to come to power and youth were the engine of his victory. Anyone who watched Obama dutifully address ten different Inauguration Balls on January 20, 2009, could see that the Youth Ball audience most energized him. Speaking to 7,000 young people he said "thank you" to a generation, explaining that his campaign was "inspired by, was energized by young people all across America."

Said the newly inaugurated president, "Young people everywhere are in process of imagining something different than what has come before us: Where there is war they imagine peace. Where there is hunger they imagine people being able to feed themselves. Where there is bigotry they imagine togetherness. The future will be in your hands if you are able to sustain the kind of energy and focus you showed on this campaign…. You are going to make it happen."

The story of the new media group described in Yes We Did is a truly amazing one. Through the internet and other digital technologies a group of young people changed just about everything: how money is raised, how people campaign, how organizers organize, and how the electorate comes to understand the issues, make choices, and become engaged in political action.

Who better to tell this striking story, and draw some lessons from it, than one of the most talented soldiers of the campaign—Rahaf Harfoush. Rather than the official account, this book is a tale from the trenches of young volunteers working with a new set of weapons and tools—the digital media.

As I studied this intersection of youth and Internet as applied to this candidate, my research suggested he was going to win. In my recent book *Grown Up Digital*, a chapter on the Obama campaign outlines the power of this combination of demographics and technology on politics, "The Net Generation and Democracy: Obama, Social Networks, and Citizen Engagement." Scarily (for my publisher) the book was finalized in August when John McCain was briefly in the lead. But my research was so compelling that I stuck to my guns and called the victory.

The modus operandi of the campaign is now being extended to governance itself, and I'm hopeful that we're in the early days of some long overdue and now possible changes in democracy itself. When President Obama announced after the inauguration that he'd ask ordinary Americans to help him change America, it didn't take long for the influencers inside the Washington beltway to ring the alarm: What happens if ordinary Americans actually come up with some new ideas to run government? Will things get out of control? Will they become bullies who will force President Obama and Congressional lawmakers to bend to their will? To me, they sound lot like the traditional marketers who are worried that they're losing control over their brand. They do have something in common. Both marketers and lawmakers are struggling to adjust to a digital world where the people out there—consumers and voters—now have the powerful tools to talk back, and even influence the brand, or the policy.

President Obama is an early pioneer in government 2.0, a new model where citizens contribute ideas to the decision-making process—to get them engaged in public life. When citizens become active, good things can happen. We all learn from each other. Initiatives get catalyzed. People become active in improving their communities, their country, and the world.

This is long overdue. These days, the policy specialists and advisers on the public-sector payroll can barely keep pace with defining the problems, let alone craft the solutions. Government can't begin to amass the in-house expertise to deal with the myriad challenges that arise. Governments need to create opportunities for sustained dialogue between voters and the elected. Courtesy of the Internet, public officials can now solicit citizen input at almost no cost, by providing web-based background information, online discussion, and feedback mechanisms.

There are lots of internet-enabled ways to engage America, from policy wikis and citizen juries to deliberative polling, ideation contests, and virtual town halls.

The goal is to have a conversation in which people become engaged in political life, think about issues, get active in improving their communities, and mobilize society for positive change. Politicians and citizens alike would become more informed and learn from each other. And collectively we would take a step away from broadcast and toward participatory democracy. As an exercise in government 2.0, it could show that power can be exercised through people, not over people.

President Obama seems to understand that a social movement of young people is not a liability, but rather something he'll need to bring about real change. This can only happen in public—not through backroom negotiations. Only through open struggle and conflict can a real and lasting change take place.

It is with great pride that I write this forward. I hired Rahaf right out of university and immediately noticed that of all the top tier talent I've hired, she was unusually capable, confident, and curious. I put her to work on my most important challenge—researching my upcoming book Wikinomics and my co-author Anthony Williams and I were equally impressed by her smarts and ability to get things done. Rahaf also energized the research and writing of my new book Grown Up Digital: How the Net Generation Is Changing Your World. I took a special interest in helping channel her big intellect and boundless energy in an optimally positive and productive direction.

However the mentoring process has become two-way. I daresay I've learned as much from her as she has from me.

Rahaf's first book is a lucid one, drawing many practical and helpful lessons for managers, marketers, and anyone trying to get things done in business or elsewhere.

Read it. Enjoy the great story and prosper. And learn how to bring about change in whatever you do.

—Don Tapscott, Toronto, March 2009

DON TAPSCOTT IS CHAIRMAN OF THE THINK TANK NGENERA INSIGHT AND THE AUTHOR OF THIRTEEN BOOKS ON THE IMPACT OF THE INTERNET ON SOCIETY. HIS LATEST IS GROWN UP DIGITAL: HOW THE NET GENERATION IS CHANGING YOUR WORLD.

INTRODUCTION

YouTube Epiphany

I don't pay much attention to email forwards. More often than not they contain amusing though useless content. When I received an email about an election-related video from a friend who had a particular fondness for forwarding photos of pets in costumes, I mentally filed it away in my *"look at later"* pile.

I reconsidered when I received a link to the same video from three different friends the following day and noticed the buzz on both Twitter and Facebook. And so, on a cold and frigid day in February 2008, I hunkered down in my Toronto apartment and headed over to YouTube to see what all the fuss was about. Shot in black and white, the video featured musical artist Will.i.am from the Black Eyed Peas accompanied by a slew of celebrities singing along to one of Senator Barack Obama's speeches. It wasn't the faces of the rich and famous that had me sitting up. It was the message of hope of and change coming from a man that until that moment I had only studied from a distance.

Woven around the refrain of "Yes We Can," Obama's concession speech from the New Hampshire primary had been put to music. I remember feeling a shiver as I watched that video. It moved me, and I shared it with all my family and friends. I was relatively unfamiliar with the Democratic candidates, with the exception of Hillary Clinton, but had been following the political race from afar as part of my research for Don Tapscott's book, *Grown Up Digital*. Barack Obama was not well known to me; I had initially discounted him as another politician in a sea of contenders. That video was a wake-up call, the catalyst that would lead me to join one of the world's most historic political campaigns.

This book isn't meant to be a "how-to" for political campaign strategy, or a biographical account of everything that happened over the past two years. Instead, my perspective will capture the role that technology played in mobilizing people to achieve real and significant change. I have documented the campaign through the eyes of social media and will discuss some of the implications and strategic insights that organizations can apply to their own brands.

The Obama campaign marks a new age of innovation that could shift the way we approach democracy itself, especially within government institutions. The team's brilliant use of technology to build relationships, transmit information, and organize offline action has redefined modern politics. Beyond that, it has permanently changed the nature of our interactions with politicians, a fact that is sure to have social and cultural implications as well.

For many organizations, this campaign has validated social media as a viable strategic tool. As new technologies continue to impact the way consumers engage with corporations, endless opportunities exist for smart executives who can leverage this new medium to create meaningful and authentic relationships. The campaign's use of blogging, social networks, text messaging, email, and video heralds a new era of integrated digital communication that is simultaneously widespread and intimate.

As the Obama administration takes office, I am savoring the global feeling of hope and change that has been absent for the last eight years. For the first time in a long time, the world is once again looking at America with respect. In the wake of a financial crisis, a war on terror that has claimed hundreds of thousands of lives, and an increasing urgency to address environmental issues, I take comfort in watching the new president's weekly YouTube address and reading the White House blog. He taps into the pioneering spirit on which North America was built—a willingness to do one's part and get to work.

We, the people, changed America. We ushered in a new age of multiculturalism, activism, and empowerment. The chorus, *"Yes We Can"* that struck me so deeply has become *"Yes We Did."* Hopefully the momentum that has begun in America will inspire similar movements around the world, as people everywhere celebrate the accomplishments of a nation that fought for change—and won.

ONE

THE UNDERDOG

THE RISE OF A MOVEMENT

1 *Introducing the Junior Senator*

THE BIRTH OF A NEW COMMUNITY

ON A CHILLY FEBRUARY DAY IN 2007, a crowd of 16,000 people applauded and cheered as Illinois Senator Barack Obama formally announced his much-anticipated presidential candidacy. He spoke eloquently about America's need for universal healthcare, ending the war in Iraq, and investing in alternative energy solutions. Standing outside the building where Abraham Lincoln had famously called on a *"house divided"* to come together, Senator Obama invoked the themes that would define the rest of his campaign: hope for a better future, the changes needed in Washington, and the part we all need to play in the process.

"If you will join me in this in improbable quest, if you feel destiny calling, and see as I see, a future of endless possibility stretching before us; if you sense, as I sense, that the time is now to shake off our slumber, and slough off our fear, and make good on the debt we owe past and future generations, then I'm ready to take up the cause, and march with you, and work with you. Together, starting today, let us finish the work that needs to be done and usher in a new birth of freedom on this Earth... That is why this campaign can't only be about me. It must be about us—it must be about what we can do together. This campaign must be the occasion, the vehicle, of your hopes, and your dreams. It will take your

time, your energy, and your advice—to push us forward when we're doing right, and to let us know when we're not. This campaign has to be about reclaiming the meaning of citizenship, restoring our sense of common purpose, and realizing that few obstacles can withstand the power of millions of voices calling for change."

BARACK OBAMA, FORMALLY ANNOUNCING HIS CANDIDACY, FEBRUARY 10, 2007,
in
Springfield, Illinois

Obama's candidacy, while welcomed by many, was considered to be a long shot. He was an African-American with a foreign-sounding name running for the country's highest office. He lacked the depth of national and executive experience held by some of his opponents. He was relatively unknown outside Illinois, and was already making statements about making big changes to the existing political system. He was up against Hillary and Bill Clinton, the quintessential power couple once described by Obama strategist David Axelrod as the *"greatest political operation in the Democratic Party."* And yet, there was something about the senator that was generating buzz online. Already groups were popping up on social networking sites like Facebook in support of his campaign. Obama's newly revamped website now featured an official blog, a campaign schedule, a video channel called BarackTV, and a social network called my.barackobama.com. A mere twenty-four hours after his announcement, 1,000 grassroots groups had already been created using the site's online tools by supporters who wanted to use the site for their own organizing.

In the early days of the race, the Obama site, particularly the blog, was geared toward putting a face on the campaign and introducing the senator to the public. A digital meet-and-greet, it featured profiles of supporters who were joining the Obama movement, and posts by key new media staffers. The tone of the blog was friendly and informal, and provided a glimpse into the inner workings of the campaign. *"About two hours after a midnight beta launch, and the site is already coming to life,"* wrote Joe Rospars, Director of New Media, in a post in February 2007. His team of nine were still tweaking the new site, excited at the activity starting to take place. *"The site is already brimming with groups, blogs, fundraising pages, and events,"* he continued. *"This site will always be a work in progress, but everyone here is excited to see what we can do together."*

In this chapter, we'll look at some of the early ways that the campaign introduced Barack Obama and started building an online community:

Tap into existing networks to amplify support — The Obama team ensured that the tools they created would appeal to existing grassroots groups, like Students for Barack Obama, who were already using the internet to organize independently.

ACTIONS SPEAK LOUDER THAN WORDS — The campaign reinforced its commitment to supporters and grassroots organizers through online initiatives such as the Donor Matching Program.

OFFER THE RIGHT INCENTIVES TO INCREASE ENGAGEMENT — Since the online community was new, the campaign had to make a concentrated effort to grow its membership and attract new donors and supporters. They did this by offering appealing incentives, including the opportunity to sit down for a dinner with Barack Obama.

PERSONALIZE THE EXPERIENCE — The Obama team always made the extra effort to add a personal touch when reaching out to the community, a tactic that differentiated them from their opponents.

Creating meaningful online relationships is an investment of time, effort, and energy. You can't rush it and you can't fake it. In gearing up to take on Hillary Clinton and John Edwards, the Obama campaign had to do several things simultaneously: encourage existing grassroots groups using sites like Facebook to migrate to the campaign's online tools, grow their online community and donor base, introduce Obama and his vision to the country, and start laying the foundation of an online grassroots movement. This was a period of growth, so mentions of opponents were limited. Instead, the dialogue revolved around building excitement about Obama's candidacy and bringing new supporters on board.

Tap into Existing Networks to Amplify Support: Students for Barack Obama

For many early supporters, my.barackobama.com became the preferred platform to continue and extend the organizing they had already been doing. It allowed them to connect with Obama supporters outside of their personal networks, and amplified their organizational efforts to an unprecedented level. Some of these groups were started even before Obama had officially declared his candidacy. One great example is Students for Obama, which was a Facebook group created in 2006 by Bowdoin College student Meredith Segal. She was so inspired by Obama's 2004 Democratic National Convention speech that she started the group to petition the senator to run for president.

The Facebook group's popularity quickly grew as thousands of new members joined the cause. When an actual campaign became a real possibility, members strategized on how they could best support Obama and turned the group into a Political Action Committee. By the time Obama officially threw his hat in the race, Students for Barack Obama had an astounding 62,000 members on Facebook and chapters on over eighty college campuses across the country. Far beyond a simple Facebook group, it had become a powerful online network of connected young people capable of using the internet to draw large crowds of supporters.

The group was so successful it was designated by the campaign as the official student organization, with Segal at the helm as executive director. Thanks to the online tools available on the Obama site, the Students for Obama movement quickly grew to over 550 campus chapters and introduced high school representatives from every state. It became one of the campaign's largest and most active online groups. Over the course of the race, Students for Barack Obama would host over 19,000 events, make 406,000 phone calls, knock on 4,500 doors, and raise $1.7 million dollars. This is just one example of many in which the Obama team used online tools to collaborate with and strengthen the efforts of existing grassroots networks.

Actions Speak Louder than Words: Counting People, Not Dollars

Part of Obama's appeal was his desire to build a new type of political campaign where regular people were empowered and involved in the democratic process. This was a message that needed to be reinforced and proven through actions, not just words. In the early days, the campaign focused on growing their online community and earning the trust of new supporters. The blogging team tackled this challenge by emphasizing the personal stories of people who had contributed to the campaign. The blog created a personal connection with readers and set a welcoming and inclusive tone for the community.

For example, take Rashed, an IT help desk specialist from Long Beach, California. He made a $5 donation, his first ever to a political campaign, which made him Obama's 75,000th contributor. To celebrate the milestone he was interviewed on the official blog and asked to share his reasons for participating in the campaign. Rashed had felt a kinship with Obama after reading the senator's book, *Dreams from My Father*. *"My dad was in the military, and I moved a lot as a child too,"* he explained. *"I remember feeling like an outsider. When I read Barack's book, I connected to it, because he moved a lot as a kid, and felt like an outsider for a while too."* Most importantly, Rashed wanted to support Barack Obama because of what he represented for his young daughter, Yasemin: the belief that she could truly accomplish anything she set her mind to. *"Now I can tell her, 'You really can be anything you want in the world.'"*

The post featured a smiling picture of Rashed and his family and made an important but subtle point. Participating in the political process, in whatever way you can, is more important than a dollar amount. Every donation makes a difference, and Rashed's story captured the spirit of giving what you can, which motivates others to participate as well. In political campaigns where traditionally only a handful of very wealthy donors were recognized for their efforts, it was refreshing to see a campaign that was focused on the stories of regular people involved in the political process. What was clever about this particular blogging initiative was the fact that Rashed's status as Obama's 75,000th donor also communicated the campaign's growing momentum. This was an important step in building credibility as a new political contender.

"I wish I could have given more, but money's very tight this month. I decided to take the money out of my son's college fund, because he's only 3 years old and I believe with all my heart that the $25 I spent today will better serve my son (and all children) going towards the senator's campaign fund than it will sitting in a bank account for 15 more years. I definitely plan on "tithing" to the cause every month, though :)"
— *Laura from Washington, D.C. (first-time donor)*

In another example, the Obama team reinforced the ethos of a community-powered campaign by letting supporters connect and share messages with each other. Nothing is more convincing or more powerful than hearing a story from someone just like you. Through a unique fundraising campaign launched in March 2007, previous donors were asked to match someone's first-time donation. Each matcher and first-time donor would have the opportunity to write a small online note to each other, explaining why this campaign was so important to them. Supporters could also include their email address to continue the conversation afterward. This turned the act of making a donation online, usually impersonal and isolating, into an opportunity to connect with someone who shared your values.

> *My husband and I struggle to make ends meet and our family is our priority but this donation can make a huge difference in our children's future. So the payback on a $10.00 has the potential to be huge!*
> — *Sandy from California (Matching Donors)*

New Media Director Joe Rospars took to the blog to explain why the campaign had chosen this method. *"We're committed to running a different kind of campaign—fueled by donations from ordinary Americans who want to take back ownership of the political process,"* he wrote. *"So this week, we're counting people, not dollars. Whether you've given before or you've been waiting for an opportunity, you can help build a campaign that's accountable to no one but the people."*

Offer the Right Incentives to Increase Engagement: Everyone Is a Special Interest

As the campaign continued to hit its fundraising goals, more enticing rewards were offered to those willing to join in the process. Angela Berg, a teacher from Sumner, Washington, became the campaign's 250,000th donor with a contribution of $100. Angela had been inspired to donate by reading the stories on the blog of people *"just like her"* who had donated. To her delight, the campaign informed her that she would have the opportunity to have a one-on-one phone call with Barack Obama himself. Her call with Obama was recorded and posted on the blog, allowing voters to hear a more casual and informal side of the senator. It showed voters that participating could make a difference and that the new face of politics was someone approachable, someone who listened and engaged with the electorate. Angela's reaction to the call was also posted on the blog. *"I can't believe it,"* she said, *"I'm so excited, not just because I got to speak with Senator Obama, but because this whole campaign is so different."* This reinforces the importance of storytelling when building an online community. It wasn't just the reward of speaking with Obama, but the resonating narrative woven around Angela's experiences that made it so effective.

For once, the spotlight was on regular Americans who, despite varied backgrounds and opinions, were united in their desire for a political process that was transparent and accessible. It was a sentiment echoed by Campaign Manager David Plouffe. *"Our funding comes from a movement of Americans giving whatever they can afford, even $5,"* he wrote in a June 6 email. *"And Barack wants to sit down with supporters like you."* Plouffe announced a new kind of fundraising dinner: during a particular week those who contributed $25 or less could have the chance to join Barack and three other donors for a sit-down dinner to discuss the issues that were affecting their communities. This was an opportunity that focused solely on small donors. Prior to the dinner, the campaign's video team was dispatched to profile each of the attendees in their hometowns and to provide a glimpse into their lives. It was a diverse group:

MARGARET THOMAS-JORDAN, a mother of two from Louisiana whose husband was serving in Iraq. • MICHAEL GRIFFITH, a miner from Nevada who had been recently laid off when his job was outsourced overseas. • CHRISTINA, a Georgia college student who donated $5 through MySpace and was concerned about environmental issues. • HAILE, a New York City Food Bank employee, founder of a nonprofit organization that creates civic programs for youth.

Each of the videos featured a person talking about how they felt Barack Obama's election would help them. This was important as it allowed people to share their enthusiasm for the campaign in their own words. The dinner itself was also taped and shared with the community, so that viewers at home could watch and see Obama's responses to the issues raised.

This type of incentive worked on several levels. By having a low barrier to entry, donors who had previously given to the campaign were more likely to donate again, and new donors could participate at a relatively low cost. It also sent a strong message that reinforced Obama's underlying philosophy: this was a movement that was possible thanks to the efforts of regular people. The Obama team catered to ordinary citizens and made their stories a focal point of the campaign. They took a perk that had traditionally been reserved for special interest groups, lobbyists, and wealthy donors and made it accessible for everyday people.

The frequency and variety of these short-term challenges, most of them lasting only one or two weeks, kept things interesting and encouraged readers to stay updated. Since the details were communicated on all of the social networks, the blog, and official email, it drove traffic to the site. Finally, because they varied in terms of the prizes and experiences, there was a greater chance to appeal to a wider audience. It made the election process seem fresh and fun and engaged people in a new way.

Personalize the Experience: Ask Yahoo!

The campaign wasn't always the first to try new things online, but they always managed to add their own special touch to anything they did. In 2007, Yahoo's community-powered knowledge market, Yahoo Answers, invited Hillary Clinton, Barack Obama, and John McCain to engage the site's 60 million members in a conversation around various issues. The site's premise was simple: users log in and ask a question which is then opened up and answered by the community.

This was the first time a tool like this was used in the political process. Hillary Clinton was the first to engage. She asked voters, *"Based on your own family's experience, what do you think we should do to improve healthcare in America?"* Over thirty-eight thousand people responded. Clinton allowed the community to vote for the best response: a user called Swbiblio who called for increased regulations for pharmaceutical companies and a plan that would provide basic healthcare for all Americans at a reasonable cost. Clinton commented on the process in her official blog, thanked users for their response, and added that she was *"moved by so many of your poignant stories, and impressed by the power and creativity of your ideas."*

Republican John McCain quickly followed and garnered over sixteen thousand responses to his question on tackling wasteful spending. He assured voters that if elected he would *"make it a top priority to balance the budget and bring fiscal discipline and accountability to a budget process that is badly broken."*

Obama was the last to approach the community, asking a question that would define the course of his campaign: *"How can we engage more people in the democratic process?"* Seventeen thousand people answered. Unlike Clinton and McCain, the Obama team selected the answer that they felt best addressed the issue. They chose a post by user "Rebecca W. in CA," who urged the candidates to link community leaders with teachers and young people to generate a lively and participatory culture of civic engagement. Instead of simply posting a response on the site, the campaign took a more personal approach: the senator called Rebecca himself and spent a few minutes chatting with her about her thoughts on engaging more people in the political process. The campaign recorded the brief conversation and made it available on the blog and on their various social network profiles.

The Yahoo Answers community received a powerful message: online action can have offline results. In this case, taking a moment to thoughtfully answer an online question got the attention of a senator and the potential future President of the United States. By choosing to address Rebecca personally, Obama was able to create an intimate dialogue with a voter, something that those who watched the video would relate to. It allowed him to infuse a touch of human contact to an otherwise cold and impersonal process, calling on his biggest strengths: eloquence and warmth.

SOCIAL MEDIA LESSONS

BUILDING ONLINE RELATIONSHIPS TAKES TIME — The campaign made the effort to slowly build relationships with its supporters. High-level campaign staff like New Media Director Joe Rospars and Campaign Manager David Plouffe were available through the blog and campaign emails to share their experience with voters. They established credibility and earned the trust of the community by backing up their words with actions: the campaign consistently put its members first.

The Obama team recognized that creating meaningful conversations is a two-way street, so they were as eager to learn about their supporters as they were to share information about themselves. The community was strengthened by the campaign's efforts to connect users to each other, and to allow them to share their own stories. They introduced Obama slowly, in phases, through phone conversations with voters and sit-down dinners. It was gradual, natural, and, most of all, expressed the authenticity of a candidate who genuinely wanted to improve the political process. Obama's phone call to Angela Berg proved to readers that this was a candidate who understood the value of reaching out to the community. This made people feel connected and instilled a sense of ownership in the political process.

TAP INTO EXISTING NETWORKS TO AMPLIFY SUPPORT — Whatever initiative you want to launch within your organization, the best place to start is to identify the existing communities that are already engaging around that particular issue. Search social networks for active groups and find online associations or communities on the web. Spend some time in these online places and listen to the conversations that are taking place. Observe how users within this community interact online and spot any area of opportunity where your social media initiative could help address an unmet need. This will provide some motivation for users to participate with your online community.

ACTIONS SPEAK LOUDER THAN WORDS — When you are launching a brand new venture, it is extremely important to build credibility and trust through actions that reinforce your value proposition. For example, if your brand is supposed to represent the highest quality of customer service, then prompt replies to comments and questions through your organization's various social networks are a great way to reinforce that reputation without having to say a word.

OFFER THE RIGHT INCENTIVES TO INCREASE ENGAGEMENT — The incentives that you offer to increase engagement are a reflection of how well you know your community members. The right incentive can be something as simple as free gear or a phone call with your CEO. Some users want "stuff," some want their ideas to be heard, and others just want their experiences validated. Identify what drives your audience and then find creative ways to deliver it. It doesn't have to be expensive—just genuine.

PERSONALIZE THE EXPERIENCE — With the increasing number of organizations deploying social media, it is highly unlikely that you will be the only representative from your industry to inhabit a particular online space. Differentiation has become increasingly important, and it can be done by simply adding a personal touch or going an extra step. From recognizing and thanking contributors in your blog's comment section, to following up with an email to make sure a customer's issue has been resolved, a personalized online experience can build a positive relationship between a consumer and brand.

ON THE CAMPAIGN TRAIL: GEARING UP

With the first few months of the campaign under their belts, the Obama team now had to prepare to go up against the Clinton machine, a daunting and intimidating foe. Further complicating matters was the fact that the first state to vote would be Iowa—a primarily white state, where the issue of race might play a big part in deciding votes. With Clinton leading in the polls, Obama had to rely on his online community to help build the grassroots network needed to challenge the New York senator—a monumental task.

2 *Up against the Clintons*

REWRITING THE RULES

"I'M IN AND I'M IN TO WIN." BOLD WORDS, SPOKEN by Hillary Clinton on the day she announced her candidacy. Her confidence was justified. With a political career spanning decades, including six years in the Senate and eight serving as First Lady, she is one of the most recognizable figures in American politics. Experienced and savvy, Clinton entered the race backed by a strong national network with deep pockets and the clout of her husband, President Bill Clinton. She also enjoyed the added advantage of being the first woman to run for president, a fact that gave her crossover appeal to Republicans and Democrats. In comparison, Obama was a junior senator with limited experience who was relatively unknown outside the state of Illinois. Clinton had been the favored front-runner since announcing her candidacy in January 2007 and continued to enjoy a healthy lead in national polls.

I will admit, initially I was a Clinton supporter. Despite some of her sharper edges, I admired Senator Clinton's tenacity and her ability to hold her own in a male-dominated arena. I respected Bill Clinton's strategic mind and considered his possible return to the White House a boon for America. What could be better than what funny-lady Tina Fey dubbed the "co-presidents?" By the time I shifted my allegiance to Obama, I had developed a healthy respect for the challenges that the Clintons would present to his campaign. Obama's underdog position necessitated an innovative approach to battle Clinton's tried-and-true tactics of traditional politics.

From an online community perspective, the Obama team had done a tremendous job both introducing Barack to supporters and creating an inclusive atmosphere among members. In this chapter, we'll take a look at how the campaign responded to Clinton's challenges and strengthened their grassroots support by using online tools to build a community that was committed, agile, and determined.

BUILDING RITUALS — The campaign constantly encouraged voters to leave their computer screens and to get involved with their community. Events such as the "Countdown to Change" parties that launched the primary and caucus season would create countless opportunities to strengthen existing bonds among supporters and reinforce the concept that online organizing would equal offline action.

DEFINING THE CONVERSATION — With the "Cost of Negativity" campaign, the Obama team framed Clinton's attacks in a way that turned her strength of traditional political strategy into a weakness.

RALLYING THE TROOPS — The "Dear Iowa" campaign created an opportunity for the entire online community to rally around a specific call to action, strengthening bonds between supporters who were using the platform.

BEING HONEST — Instead of glossing over the New Hampshire loss, the campaign opened up to supporters in an email that outlined the challenges ahead and spurred grassroots groups into action.

Building Rituals: Countdown to Change

In early September 2007, the campaign's focus was on the early-state primaries and caucuses coming up in January 2008. The Obama team started laying the groundwork for offline participation. Through social network profile updates, blog posts, and emails from David Plouffe, supporters were encouraged to either host or attend a "Countdown to Change" party to kick off the upcoming primaries and caucuses in Iowa, New Hampshire, Nevada, and South Carolina. *"Now is the time to leverage our national movement to make the maximum impact in the early states,"* wrote Plouffe. *"We can only win in these essential contests if our strongest supporters combine their efforts across the country."*

The goal of the parties was to establish a precedent of on-the-ground action. Supporters were encouraged to get together and discuss how they could prepare for the upcoming primaries and caucuses. Attendees from across the country were able to participate in an exclusive conference call with staff who were currently working in the four early states. This gave them an insider's look at the campaign's preparations. The emails, social networks, and blogs all directed users to the same place: an interactive map on barackobama.com that would help supporters find watch parties in their neighborhoods. The Obama site also provided host guides, to help supporters plan, promote and run their events. Users could sign up and share the event with others. The conference calls were recorded and uploaded to the blog so that those who missed the date would still be in the loop.

The house party campaign was essential because it laid the groundwork for linking online organizing to offline activity. It forced people to engage with the site and familiarize themselves with the tools and applications early on. It also provided a good reason for supporters to come face to face and meet each other, an act that would strengthen community bonds and build networks that would be essential to later organizing.

Defining the Conversation: The Cost of Negativity

Clinton's team pulled no punches and aggressively attacked Obama on multiple fronts, including his lack of experience. The Obama campaign responded by claiming the tone of Clinton's ads were evidence of a broken political process. They stated that negative attacks had no place in discussions about America's future. On December 3, 2007, Campaign Manager David Plouffe sent out a scathing email harpooning Clinton's negative advertising strategy. He shared the latest Iowa polls, which showed that Obama had taken the lead, even among women. *"Iowans have found that Senator Clinton is running the most negative campaign of any candidate,"* he wrote. *"These attacks take attention away from solving people's problems and exact a real cost on our political process."*

Plouffe suggested that the appropriate response would be to increase the cost of these tactics by showing strength in the face of such negativity. In a brilliant move, he turned Clinton's ad campaign into an opportunity for supporters to make a statement about the dark and aggressive nature of current politics. *"The Cost of Negativity"* was an online campaign that called for 10,000 people to donate $25 within a 48-hour period, proving that when opponents *"attack Barack Obama it will literally make our campaign stronger."*

This initiative turned Clinton's knowledge of traditional campaign strategy against her. *"Senator Clinton's personal attacks come from the same, tired textbook of establishment politics,"* continued Plouffe. The email concluded with a link to a video that showcased Iowans explaining why they were supporting Barack. The video ended on a hopeful note that resonated with viewers who not only wanted a different and more hopeful America, but also wanted a better process to help them get there. The initiative was hugely successful, and the campaign easily surpassed its goal of 10,000 supporters.

When the Clinton campaign refused to change tactics, the Obama camp intensified the pressure by launching a site entitled "Hillary Attacks" that tracked the Senator's negative ads. The site encouraged voters to *"be vigilant and notify us immediately of any attacks from Senator Clinton or her supporters as soon as you seem them so that we can respond with the truth swiftly and forcefully."* Supporters could subscribe to the Obama Supporter Rapid Response team, a list that could be mobilized  via email to take action against a Clinton attack by writing letters to newspapers or television stations.

These tactics allowed the Obama campaign to gain control and define the conversation. By asking supporters to be on the lookout for any negativity from Clinton, they would search for negative meaning in everything that she said. The campaign was able to criticize Clinton's actions without resorting to personal attacks, giving them the high ground of integrity. They also used Clinton's ads to start a dialogue by highlighting the shortcomings of the current debate process, making anything Clinton said or did seem outdated and a part of the Washington status quo. Through the rapid response squad, the emails, and the Hillary Attacks website, the campaign was able to use new media to bypass traditional press outlets and speak directly with voters, allowing them to better control the conversation. They were able to rebrand Obama from inexperienced newcomer to agent of change, someone who would infuse new energy into a tired process.

Rallying the Troops: Dear Iowa

As the Iowa caucus loomed on January 3, 2008, the need for on-the ground support intensified. There was a big online push to recruit

precinct captains, people who would take responsibility for a group of neighborhoods and help drive voter registrations and candidate awareness. The blog and emails started featuring testimonials of precinct captains who explained why they had decided to join the campaign and urged others to do the same.

This movement had always been about community. Supporters not only connected with Obama, they had to connect with each other as well. The "Dear Iowa" program was an online community-wide effort where supporters from across the country could login to barackobama.com and write a note of encouragement to Iowa precinct captains and volunteers, thanking them for their hard work. Iowa state blogger Sarah Ramey posted about the impact of such campaigns. *"Precinct captains all over Iowa are feeling the love,"* she wrote. *"Over 20,000 letters of support have arrived from around the country, encouraging them to keep up the great work here in the homestretch."*

The Obama blog also featured examples of some of the messages, reinforcing the camaraderie that was blooming among supporters. This was effective because it allowed community members to express their feelings about the campaign in their own words and share them with other supporters. It provided an opportunity for people to get involved in the process by writing notes of support, a small and easy gesture that had a tangible impact. For those on the receiving end, the notes emphasized the importance of their role. This initiative increased the precinct captains' feelings of ownership and accountability to the campaign, since they knew that supporters were counting on them to succeed. As the campaign became more personal, volunteers were increasingly invested in the outcome and determined to see it through.

The campaign's online organizing efforts would pay off. After months of trailing Clinton and battling issues of race, something incredible happened: a decisive victory for Obama in Iowa! Obama claimed 38 percent of the vote, followed by Edwards at 30 percent and Clinton with 29 percent. For Clinton, despite having won an equal number of delegates, the loss was a blow to her indomitable front-runner image. *"This race begins tonight and ends when Democrats throughout America have their say,"* she told supporters. *"Our campaign was built for a marathon."*

Obama's unlikely win captured the attention of voters and lent credibility to the movement of change he was championing. The sheer number of Democrats who turned out was a statement in itself: 236,000 people— nearly double the attendance of the 2004 caucus. In practical terms, it proved that online organizing could in fact lead to offline action. The victory was attributed to voters who weren't traditionally known for turning up at the caucuses: Republicans, independents, young people—all

"I think that this is my generation's moment. This is our chance to right the wrongs that decades of politics as usual has created. Thank you for supporting Barack, you are doing me and our country proud."
—*Tyler in Ohio*

"For the first time, I feel hope and excitement for a Presidential race—hope that we can not only want change, but demand it. You are a part of that hope, so I thank you for the time and sacrifice you have made."
—*Kelly in Idaho*

"In this election, we can choose whether we want to continue to live in fear, or reach for what we know is possible, a strong, confident and positive America our children will grow up in and the world will look up to."
—*Yiannis in Maryland*

were inspired by Obama to make their voices heard. *New York Times* columnist David Brooks wrote, *"This is a huge moment. It's one of those times when a movement that seemed ethereal and idealistic became a reality and took on political substance."*

This success alleviated some of the concern about investing heavily  in the online community without any true predictions of how online participation would translate into action at critical junctures. It was important for the new online community to strengthen its bond and reinforce its mandate with a collective goal. Writing an online note was an easy way support the campaign that was free, fast, and instantly made you feel better. Online community members felt connected to a bigger movement and would be more likely to take part in future initiatives.

"Years from now, you'll look back and you'll say that this was the moment—this was the place—where America remembered what it means to hope... This was the moment when we tore down barriers that have divided us for too long—when we rallied people of all parties and ages to a common cause; when we finally gave Americans who'd never participated in politics a reason to stand up and to do so."
—Barack Obama, Victory Speech, Iowa

Being Honest:
The New Hampshire Gamble

After a few posts celebrating the Iowa win, the blog quickly geared up for the next challenge: the New Hampshire primary taking place on January 8, 2008. Plouffe spoke to the *Concord Monitor* about the campaign's strategy. *"Historically, New Hampshire has been a very* important primary and obviously it's going to impact the states to come later down the road, including Nevada, South Carolina, and the February 5 states," he said. "We're talking to thousands of voters every night and every afternoon. The ground campaign in New Hampshire is ferocious right now." Accompanied by volunteers, a field staff of 100 had knocked on 300,000 doors. Things were looking good. Spirits were still high from the Iowa win and there was a growing hope that a similar outcome in New Hampshire could propel Obama to the lead. This optimism was further bolstered by Obama's ability to draw record crowds at rallies and a healthy lead in New Hampshire polls, where in some cases he was ahead by ten points.

Then something unexpected happened.

Senator Clinton's emotional and teary-eyed response to a voter question on the day before the primary revealed a softer side to the usually stoic woman. This sparked a media frenzy of commentary where reactions spanned the spectrum of emotions including sympathy, skepticism, and even suspicion. However, she had struck a nerve with the public, resulting in an outpouring of support from voters, particularly women, who rallied around her.

Clinton defied all predictions by winning 39 percent of the New Hampshire vote, followed by Obama at 36 percent. The loss would be a heavy blow to the confidence of the Obama team who had entered the primary as the front-runner. It ended any notion of a quick and tidy victory and meant several more months of grueling campaigning lay ahead. The battle would be long and weary, a sentiment that seemed to permeate an email sent by David Plouffe on January 9, 2008. Frank and to the point, the email outlined the steps needed to survive the next round of campaigning. "Our campaign now turns its focus squarely to Nevada and South Carolina, and February 5. Today, we kick off the next phase of our campaign in New Jersey," Plouffe wrote to supporters.

Instead of glossing over the loss, Plouffe took a decidedly different approach. In a campaign first, he included an update of fundraising and campaigning status. The email read like an internal memo and effectively laid out the campaign's strategy for the next few weeks. Readers were briefed on the current number of donors, funds raised, and where the money would be spent. Despite the loss, Obama and Clinton were still tied in terms of pledged delegates, and the email ended on a positive note. Fundraising was going well, and predictions indicated the campaign would see an increase in both new donors and dollars raised. *"We continue to build a grassroots movement that makes us best-positioned to compete financially in the primaries and caucuses coming up,"* he wrote. The email was so well received by readers that similar information would be incorporated into future communications.

By using the primary loss as an opportunity to speak frankly to their community, the campaign transformed a demoralizing event into a bonding experience, as members felt included and empowered to play their part. This was good news for the Obama team because with the long fight ahead, they would need to rely heavily on their grassroots organizers.

In the remaining early contests, Obama would win South Carolina while Clinton would claim Nevada; neither side would be able to gain the lead heading into Super Tuesday.

WHERE OBAMA STANDS

In a blog series entitled "Where Obama Stands," official campaign bloggers reviewed Barack's policies on a particular issue, taking the time to outline the current problem as well as his proposed solutions.

NATIONAL VOTER PROTECTION CENTER

The campaign launched the National Voter Protection Center, an online site designed to educate voters about their rights along with a hot-line number they could call to speak to lawyers in case they encountered any issues or problems at the polls.

SOCIAL NETWORKING IN ACTION

Joey Bristol was the first campaign staffer sent to Idaho to officially organize for Obama. When he arrived, Bristol was greeted by Idaho for Obama, a local grassroots group whose 100 members had already been aggressively organizing field operations. They had taken the liberty of scheduling meetings for Bristol with important community leaders and had already formed subgroups in counties all across the state.

SOCIAL MEDIA LESSONS

BUILDING RITUALS — Newly launched communities need to establish routines and rituals in order to manage user expectations and lay the foundation for future engagement. Rituals can include anything from a weekly blog to a monthly giveaway, anything that helps build a sense of online community and that forges a connection between your organization and consumers.

DEFINING THE CONVERSATION — Social media allows your organization to bypass traditional news cycles and engage in direct conversations with your consumers. This presents a powerful platform where you can share your side of the story.

RALLYING THE TROOPS — Nothing brings people together faster than uniting around a common cause. Whether it is a new product that will add value to consumers or supporting a local cause, involving the online community in achieving a goal is a great way to build relationships. You can ask consumers to show their support by asking them to Twitter about the issue, providing online badges they can place on their blog or social network profiles, or inviting them to sign an online petition. Whatever the method, ensure that it makes the community feel united in facing the issue together.

BEING HONEST — We tend to forget that behind big corporations there are people just like us, prone to making mistakes now and then. One of the advantages of social media is how fast an organization can address a misstep. A response issued within hours, rather than days, can quickly defuse a potentially volatile situation. The most important thing to remember when addressing your online audience is to be honest and frank about the situation at hand. Denying a mistake or using traditional spin will erode any trust that has been built and damage your brand's reputation.

ON THE CAMPAIGN TRAIL:
FEBRUARY 2008—SUPER TUESDAY

The campaign was now heading into Super Tuesday 2008: on February 5, twenty-three states would hold primaries or caucuses. With so many elections happening simultaneously, the Obama team needed to strategize about where to allocate resources. Despite drawing a record number of attendees at his events and support from the likes of Oprah Winfrey and Ted and Caroline Kennedy, Obama found himself in a dead heat with Clinton. With 1,681 delegates up for grabs and Clinton polling well in several states, the campaign had to readjust its game plan.

The Obama team decided to target small caucus states where Clinton had little to no presence, such as Idaho. The move was risky, and would require more manpower than current campaign resources allowed. They would have to depend on the online organizing ability of their community. *"It was the first time that we took an enormous leap of faith in our online grassroots network that was already out there,"* said National Field Director Jon Carson. People from across the country rose to the challenge. In Tennessee, over 200 supporters showed up for the grand opening of the state headquarters ready to canvass and make calls on behalf of Obama. Volunteers used the internet to create sophisticated networks of grassroots groups months before an official campaign presence arrived.

On Super Tuesday, Obama won 13 states and territories. In states like Idaho, where online organizing had played a big part, Obama won by wide margins. Clinton won 10 states including electoral heavyweights California and Massachusetts. Overall, Obama won 847 pledges to Clinton's 834. Once again confounding those who had predicted a clear winner after Super Tuesday, the candidates found themselves in a tie. The rest of February would bring an additional 11 elections, and Obama would win them all, leading in pledged delegates as well as the national popular vote. By March the Obama campaign would count 1,192 delegates to Clinton's 1,035. However, Clinton's campaign was still leading in the number of superdelegates: she had 240 compared to Obama's 191.

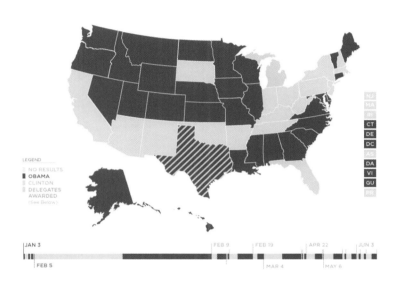

LEGEND

NO RESULTS
OBAMA
CLINTON
DELEGATES
AWARDED
(See Below)

NJ
MA
RI
CT
DE
DC
AS
DA
VI
GU
PR

JAN 3

FEB 9

FEB 19

APR 22

JUN 3

FEB 5

MAR 4

MAY 6

3 *The Road to Denver*

NAVIGATING CONTROVERSY

ON MARCH 4, 2008 WAS THE DATE THAT
primaries and caucuses would be held in four states: Ohio, Rhode
Island, Texas, and Vermont. With 370 delegates up for grabs, the
"Mini-Super Tuesday" could play a critical role in deciding the
next Democratic nominee. Ohio's working-class population and
the Texas Latino community were powerful voters who tended to
favor Clinton, giving the New York senator a double-digit lead in
the polls. Seeing an opportunity to break their perpetual tie, Clinton
unleashed an offensive strategy, attacking Obama on multiple fronts.
From humorously poking fun of Obama's favorable media coverage
on *Saturday Night Live*, to seriously questioning his ability to lead in
a crisis, she was determined to maintain her lead.

With the National Democratic Convention taking place in August,
the pressure intensified. The next few months were turbulent for the
Obama team as Clinton proved to be an unyielding foe. This chapter
examines how they skillfully navigated through controversy using
their online community and new media tools.

THE POWER OF SMALL ASKS — The campaign asked supporters to complete one small task—make five calls using the online phonebanking
tool to achieve a goal—and was rewarded by an unprecedented
volume of community involvement.

LET YOUR ADVOCATES SUPPORT YOU — The controversial footage of
Reverend Jeremiah Wright's inflammatory remarks would be one of
Obama's biggest tests. By opening up such a sensitive subject to the
community and encouraging discussions about a volatile topic, the
Obama team turned voters into advocates who would speak up and
defend the senator.

LEAD BY EXAMPLE — As it became more evident that Barack Obama was
seen as the presumptive nominee, the campaign realized it needed to
build a bridge with Clinton supporters. By officially welcoming her
into the community, they encouraged supporters to do the same.

DEPUTIZE THE WILLING — By identifying those who were most passionate about the campaign, the Obama team was able to delegate some of its most important work to a select group of capable and willing supporters.

The Power of Small Asks and Big Names: Make Five Calls

The campaign's online phonebanking tool enabled supporters to access voter lists and make calls for Obama. The premise was simple: to access the tool, supporters logged in to my.barackobama.com, the official social network, to join a calling campaign targeting a specific state. This allowed supporters to make calls from their home instead of having to go into a campaign field office in person. Obama volunteers were reaching out to voters, encouraging them to vote and get involved in the campaign. The tool had already been used to make 700,000 calls but that still wasn't impacting Clinton's lead. The Obama team once again found itself at a make-or-break moment and was facing the possibility of losing the nomination to Clinton. They rallied the online community in an effort to survive this latest round. The campaign set a goal of using the online phonebanking tool to make 300,000 more phone calls to convince voters in Ohio, Rhode Island, Texas, and Vermont to vote for Obama on March 4.

MAKE THE CALL

If they were successful, the 300,000 additional calls would push the campaign's total call count to an impressive one million. The situation was grave enough to warrant an email from Barack. "*I*

need you to make your voice heard today, literally," he wrote on March 1, 2008. *"We've set a goal of one million calls to help Get Out the Vote for these critical states—will you help?"* The blog and social network profiles began publishing posts of encouragement, updating readers with an hourly tally of the calls made. Supporters who wanted to get involved were asked to start with one small action: make five calls.

Making 300,000 phone calls in four days was an ambitious goal. Incredibly, the Obama campaign passed the million-phone-call mark within twenty-four hours of Obama's call to action. With three days still remaining, the campaign increased their goal by an additional 500,000 calls for a total of 1.5 million calls into election states. *"You are the voice of this campaign, and there are thousands of people out there, waiting to hear from you,"* wrote David Plouffe in a follow-up email. Once again, the blog posts pushed the new goal and encouraged everyone to make *"just five more calls."*

For many volunteers, this was their first time participating in a political campaign, let alone phonebanking. *"I've never done something like this before,"* wrote one supporter in the blog comments, *"but five calls seems like such a small way to help bring about big change that I couldn't say no."* Calls poured in. 1.5 million calls were made within 48 hours of setting the new goal. A total of 2,049,133 calls were made using the online phonebanking tool in the days leading up to the March 4 primaries and caucuses. Clinton won Ohio, Rhode Island, and the Texas primary, while Obama took the Texas caucus and the Vermont primary.

Surprisingly, despite Clinton's victories, Obama received enough delegates to keep him in the race, and her delegate gains were effectively canceled out by Obama's victories in Wyoming and Mississippi a few days later. Once again the two candidates were neck and neck, with 210 pledged delegates for Obama and 205 for Clinton. Thanks to the incredible volume of calls made by supporters into voting states, the Obama campaign emerged from a critical battle relatively unscathed, and leading in the delegate count. The campaign didn't ask voters to make ten or twenty calls; they asked each person to make just five phone calls. Five is an unintimidating number that helped supporters feel empowered without being overwhelmed.

Let Your Advocates Support You:
A More Perfect Union

With the Pennsylvania primary six weeks away, the
Obama team faced one of
its largest controversies to
date. Reverend Jeremiah
Wright, Obama's former
pastor, had been videotaped
making radical statements
during a sermon. The
footage had surfaced on
YouTube and was picked up
by the mainstream media.
As the negative press coverage increased, so did
the pressure for Obama
to denounce the man who
had officiated his wedding
and baptized his children.

INDIANA'S 3-ON-3 CHALLENGE FOR CHANGE:

Any student in Indiana who registered
at least 20 of their friends to vote qual-
ified to be chosen by the campaign to
play a game of 3-on-3 basketball with
two of their friends against Barack
Obama.

Highlights of the game were videotaped and uploaded on the blog and
social network sites. Obama's team
defeated his opponents 15-5. The
senator scored four baskets, made two
steals, caught four rebounds, and had
one assist.

The voter registration drive was also
a success, adding 150,000 new voters
in Indiana.

A YouTube video statement from Barack Obama rejecting the
inflammatory statements made by Wright did not seem to appease
the public nor stop the pundits from dissecting Wright's influence
on Obama. The Obama website did not directly mention the Wright
incident again. Four days later Obama addressed the nation with
a 37-minute speech titled "A MORE PERFECT UNION" that would
become a defining moment not only for the campaign, but also for
American politics in general.

Instead of shying away from the uncomfortable topic of race relations,
Obama faced it head on, framing Wright's comments within a socio-
logical and historical context that revealed the darker prejudices still
lurking in the United States. He called on Americans to move beyond
the "racial stalemate" if they wanted to tackle the social issues that
affected all of them. "A MORE PERFECT UNION" managed to condemn
Wright's comments without shunning the man himself. A report
released by the Pew Research Center described it as "arguably the
biggest political event of the campaign so far," and found that 85
percent of Americans had heard about the speech. On YouTube,

the video generated 3.4 million views in the first ten days alone. It quickly went viral and popped up on blogs and social networks, and was forwarded in emails across the country.

The Obama team saw an opportunity to help encourage dialogue and posted the video of "A MORE PERFECT UNION," including the entire text, on the blog and on the various social networks. In addition, campaign bloggers included the reactions of both the press and members of the public, and invited the submission of comments and reactions. The blog became a rich and supportive discussion where people from all backgrounds shared their views.

> *"My family, in total, like Barack's, has all races, all religions, and more personalities and imperfections than can be listed. I have supported this campaign from the beginning, and have struggled to articulate to others the profound integrity that I feel Barack Obama has. Luckily for me, this speech says it all. He can and we can, and together we all can make this country great!"*
> —*Wendy H. in Golden, Colorado*

> *"I will be voting in the Indiana primary in May and I look forward to voting for Senator Obama."*
> —*Christina M. in Lawrenceburg, Indiana*

The campaign was able to discuss Obama's speech and its emotional impact on voters without having to mention the Wright controversy at all. Obama elevated the issue into a broader platform for dialogue and let his advocates defend and support him online. He turned a controversy into an opportunity to connect with the community that strengthened his voter base and attracted new supporters who were moved by the speech to get involved.

MEDIA REACTION

"The best speech and most important speech on race that we have heard as a nation since Martin Luther King's 'I HAVE A DREAM' speech."
—*Michelle Bernard, MSNBC Political Analyst*

"Barack Obama didn't simply touch the touchiest subject in America, he grabbed it and turned it over and examined it from several different angles and made it personal. Just steps from Independence Hall in Philadelphia, he rang the bell hard and well."
—*Jonathan Alter,* Newsweek *Senior Editor and Columnist*

Lead by Example: Welcome Hillary Supporters

Despite Clinton's win in Pennsylvania and Indiana, Obama's victory in North Carolina on May 6, 2008, had him ahead by 164 delegates. He continued to receive endorsements from superdelegates. In May he surpassed Clinton's superdelegate total for the first time, edging into the lead. Clinton refused to give up, and scored convincing wins in West Virginia and Kentucky. The fight continued in Oregon, where Obama's victory finally gained him the needed pledges to unofficially clinch the nomination, ending a long and exhausting fight.

He returned to Des Moines, Iowa, for his victory speech. *"The road here has been long, there have been bumps along the way. I have made some mistakes, but also it's partly because we've traveled this road with one of the most formidable candidates to ever run for this office,"* he said to a cheering crowd. *"Now, some may see the millions upon millions of votes cast for each of us as evidence that our party is divided, but I see it as proof that we have never been more energized and united in our desire to take this country in a new direction."* Comments of support and celebration from social networks across the web were featured on the blog, along with the footage of Obama's victory speech.

In the final primaries in Montana and South Dakota in June 2008, Obama added the endorsement of another sixty superdelegates. On June 7, after seventeen months of grueling battle and close calls, Clinton officially suspended her campaign and endorsed Obama. The junior senator from Illinois had managed to become the Democratic nominee in the race to be the President of the United States of America.

Amidst their victory, the campaign now faced another situation where they had to tread carefully. The race between Clinton and

Obama had been hard-fought and was often heated. Many Clinton supporters were so upset at her loss that they threatened to vote Republican instead of supporting Obama, an unusual situation for the Democratic Party. Facing an equally tough battle against John McCain, the Obama campaign needed to shore up all the Democratic support possible, and that meant extending the olive branch to Clinton supporters.

The Obama team made a concentrated effort to create a welcoming online environment. For example, online members were invited to write a message to Senator Clinton, thanking her for her candidacy and endorsement. This was an essential part of community building and indicated a fresh start and a new conciliatory relationship with Clinton. Campaign blogger Christopher Hass shared some of the messages coming in. *"All day yesterday and today, we've heard from thousands of people who have shared their thanks and thoughts with Senator Hillary Clinton as this incredible primary draws to a close,"* he wrote. *"We've seen Obama supporters expressing their admiration for Senator Clinton, Clinton supporters declaring their support in the general election for Barack, and people on both sides taking pause to acknowledge the historic nature of this seventeen-month contest."*

Those words established a message of friendly intent that members of the community carried forward. By setting the social cues online, the campaign made it very clear what behaviors were expected

and how Clinton supporters were to be treated online. By showing the online community how to act instead of merely instructing them to do so, the campaign was able to communicate a genuine and sincere message to Clinton supporters. This goodwill was echoed by the community and paved the way for positive interactions online, including the creation of several groups welcoming Clinton supporters to the Obama social network.

MESSAGES TO HILLARY

"It has been a long tough fight for us all. Most importantly it has been historic. You and Barack have broken down many doors. Now that we move forward to the general election and John McCain, I expect nothing more than the tough, hard hitting fighter that you have always been."
—Cee from Maryland

"Dear Hillary, Thank you so much for your outstanding example of what we as women can do if we strive to. Thank you for such a warm, kind, yet powerful endorsement of Barack Obama."
—Catherine from Illinois

"I am a former Hillary supporter (still am)... but after watching her today, I was motivated to throw my support to Obama, because we do not need another Republican. I hope and I pray that people in the Obama camp are warm towards the Hillary supporters, because we were all passionate for her, just like the Obama supporters are for him. Let's all please just get along and realize the history in the making. I LOVE YOU HILLARY and THANK YOU for proving that women can do it too!"
—Arlene from California

WELCOME HILLARY
SUPPORTERS 4 OBAMA

212 MEMBERS

830 EVENTS HOSTED

6,828 EVENTS ATTENDED

15,825 CALLS MADE

760 DOORS KNOCKED ON

9,486 BLOG POSTS

$34,933.58 RAISED

"Senator Clinton. Thank you. I saw all my Hillary support-ing friends last night and they all came up to hug me and in unison screamed 'YES WE CAN!' Oh happy day!"
—Sherry in Minnesota

Deputize the Willing: The Obama Fellows

The next milestone was the Democratic National Convention in Denver, Colorado, where Obama would officially accept the nomina-

tion. While the convention was still ten weeks away, the Obama campaign continued to push its online organizing efforts, intensifying volunteer training and recruitment. The Obama Fellowship Program was an opportunity for dedicated volunteers to prepare for the general election. Created to embody Obama's philosophy that profound change has to come from the ground up, the unpaid program ran for six weeks, including one week of intensive training. Fellows were divided into regional teams and trained in phonebanking, canvassing, voter registration, and grassroots organizing. The goal was clear: build a base of volunteers and voters for the general election and train them to use the online tools.

The fellowship was not an army that any warm body could join, but an honored distinction. Fellows were carefully screened and chosen based on their resume, previous campaign-related experience, letters of reference, and their written answers to the following questions:

Everyone has a unique story that brings them to this movement for change. Why are you personally motivated to be involved in this campaign?

One of Senator Obama's first jobs was to organize in the South Side of Chicago and register voters in the community. Please tell us if you have any experience as an organizer, either community organizing or political organizing.

If you have been working with the campaign, please describe your activities (types, dates, locations) and what you have learned. If you have not been involved with the campaign yet, please describe why you have decided to get involved now.

FIGHT THE SMEARS

In June 2008, the campaign launched a new site called Fightthesmears.com that armed supporters with the information they needed to debunk some of the rumors and smears that had been circulating online. The site provided an email address (watchdog@ barackobama.com) for supporters to report any smears they had received. It also invited them to join the Action Wire, a mailing list where subscriberscould register breaking news and urgent calls to action to address some of these smears. The Action Wire had a presence on MySpace and Facebook, and blog badges were available as well.

Fellows committed to a six-week unpaid assignment and had to cover their own transportation, housing, and living costs. Accommodation with other Obama supporters was a possibility, but nothing was guaranteed. The fellows were deployed all over the country in units consisting of a coordinator, data manager, volunteer coordinator, voter registration and contact coordinator, and a house meeting coordinator. Over the course of their term, fellows worked with campaign staff and grassroots leaders to build relationships with citizens. In communities across the country they trained supporters on the online tools, helping to create strong networks that would be self-sufficient after they left. In addition to voter outreach, fellow responsibilities included writing letters to the editor, walking in parades, putting up lawn signs, representing the campaign at community gatherings, helping with Get Out the Vote (GOTV) initiatives, and various administrative tasks. The focus was to reinforce online organizing with offline action.

Over the course of the summer, over 3,600 fellows were dispatched into seventeen states to train and recruit new volunteers. The Obama blog dutifully reported on the fellows, introducing a series called "Organizing Fellows" that featured profiles on the fellows as they completed their assignments. Obama blogging staff did an exemplary job in building up a compelling narrative that delved into the backgrounds and motivations of each person who had volunteered for this program.

"I got my chance on the South Side of Chicago, as a community organizer, and it was the transformative experience of my career.

It allowed me to put my values to work and to see that real change comes not from the top-down, but from the bottom-up, when ordinary people come together around a common purpose. The experience changed the course of my life—and I want to share that kind of opportunity with you."
—Barack Obama, Email to Supporters, April 3, 2008

SOCIAL MEDIA LESSONS

THE POWER OF SMALL ASKS — Internet users are bombarded with all sorts of asks on a daily basis: fill out this survey, watch this video, comment on this blog. It can be overwhelming. If you want consumers to engage with your content, especially if you are new in this space or have yet to build a substantial following, the key is to start with something simple. Instead of a survey, try a one-question poll. The easier and less time-consuming you make the task, the more likely people will participate. One common misstep on corporate blogs is forcing the visitor to register for a membership before he or she can comment on the content.

LET YOUR ADVOCATES SUPPORT YOU — Engaged community members will tirelessly defend their favorite brands. They will blog in response to negative press and make statements you could never make as an organization—no matter how much you want to. They will also defend you in battles that you might not even know are happening, on the far reaches of obscure forums and personal Facebook walls. The key is to leverage your advocates and highlight their support for others to see. You can do this by actively promoting your biggest fans. Linking to their sites, acknowledging their comments, and engaging with them in an authentic manner will build trust and loyalty.

LEAD BY EXAMPLE — People are always searching for cues to indicate how they should act in social situations. Online communities are no different. This is particularly important if your social media initiative involves a platform for discussion such as a forum board, wall, or blog comment section. Enforcing terms of service that outline appropriate behavior will ensure that community members fully understand the appropriate way to engage with each other.

DEPUTIZE THE WILLING — A community can take a lot of work to build. It requires time and effort, and for many organizations resources can be an issue. One solution is to identify your most active community member and deputize him or her with an official role. From a discussion moderator to a content generator, passionate people will engage with a cause they care about, especially if they feel their contributions are valued. This move isn't without risk. Inviting someone to take ownership and help manage your community means giving them a say and listening to their suggestions and feedback—even if it's something you don't want to hear. Smart managers will recognize the immense value in this feedback and will make sure that proper processes are in place to evaluate and act on the ideas that are presented. Nurture your most active contributors and they will nurture your brand.

ON THE CAMPAIGN TRAIL

August 2008 brought the online community to maturity. Since 2007, the community had grown from a newly formed community to an organized and powerful national grassroots network. With the Democratic nomination officially secured, Barack Obama, who started the race as the long shot, was transformed into the candidate, a political powerhouse capable of rallying millions of people to organize on his behalf. He announced Senator Joe Biden as his running mate through a text message sent to subscribers before it was shared with the press. As the convention drew closer, subtle transformations began to occur on the website and blog as the Obama brand was polished and refined. It was as though the official site had become secure in its identity and was fully ready to challenge John McCain and the Republican Party.

4 *Understanding the Past*

THE HISTORY OF ONLINE CAMPAIGNING

AMID ALL THE EXCITEMENT AND AWE that surrounded this revolutionary campaign, people sometimes overlook the fact that Obama's achievements were made possible by the initiative, resourcefulness, and experiences of those who came before him. Innovation happens gradually, and is often punctuated by bursts of disruptive technology that level the playing field, create new markets, and change the way people interact.

While this book focuses on new media strategy, it is important to understand the political and technological contexts surrounding the 2008 election to accurately evaluate the campaign's success. The strategic decisions made by Obama and his team created conditions that fostered an agile and flexible social media plan. They validated the importance of new media by making it a stand-alone department instead of an add-on to the communications team. This campaign was run differently from the start and new media's innovative spirit is a natural extension of that mindset.

The success of the Obama campaign comes down to refinement—not invention. The team improved upon existing new media tools to build a scalable organization with national reach that allowed the Democrats to compete in areas they had been unable to penetrate before. The campaign's ability to deliver customized messaging to supporters (see Chapter 9) was built on statistical techniques initially pioneered by George Bush's 2004 reelection campaign. The social network strategy that guided the development of the Obama social network (see Chapter 6, My.BarackObama.com) was built on the foresight of people like Howard Dean who saw the internet's potential for effective organizing.

In this chapter, we'll look at some of the important technological innovations that made many aspects of the campaign possible and examine the political decisions that allowed the Obama team to be innovative with their social media strategy.

CREATING CUSTOMIZED MESSAGING — George W. Bush's 2004 reelection campaign introduced microtargeting as a statistical tool to identify voter demographics and craft a communications strategy.

ONLINE ORGANIZING — Howard Dean saw the potential in using the internet to organize his supporters, but could not translate online enthusiasm into offline action.

EMERGENCE OF NEW TECHNOLOGIES — MoveOn.org fused microtargeting with online phonebanking to create a new campaign tool.

THE INNOVATION CONTEXT — The Obama campaign adopted the Fifty-State Strategy, targeted the disaffected center of the Democratic Party, and focused on small donors; these decisions led to the creation of an integrated new media strategy.

Creating Customized Messaging: The 2004 George Bush Re-election Campaign

In 2002, the Bush Administration was considering strategies for the upcoming 2004 reelection. Republican Senior Strategist Karl Rove received an interesting pitch by a research consultant named Alexander Gage, who wanted to apply the same microtargeting techniques used to segment consumers for corporations to Bush's reelection campaign. Microtargeting uses a statistical technique called predictive market segmentation to identify groups of similar individuals and extrapolate their patterns of behavior. By examining trends in income, family status, occupation, and other data, the Bush campaign could discover segments of overlooked voters and create a tailored communication strategy to address their needs.

Pioneered by Gage's firm, TargetPoint Consulting, microtargeting had never before been used in a national political campaign. Rove was intrigued, but wanted proof. Gage was asked to predict how different population segments would vote in several Pennsylvania judicial races, a task he completed with 90 percent accuracy. Satisfied, the Bush campaign enlisted Gage to analyze and microtarget battleground states and used his findings to craft their strategy. It was a highly successful tactic that provided the Bush campaign with new population segments of likely Bush voters. For example, they were able to contact 92 percent of eventual Bush voters in Iowa and 84 percent of Bush voters in Florida, compared with 50 percent in each state during the 2000 election. The Obama campaign would apply these techniques to their email strategy and create hypersegmented emails that provided readers with customized messaging.

Online Organizing: The 2004 Howard Dean Campaign

While the Republicans were revolutionizing the application of statistics in politics, the Democrats were tackling the issue of voter outreach from a different angle: online organizing. Leading the pack was Howard Dean, whose approach would lay the foundation for Obama's unprecedented online grassroots movement. Dean supporters used Meetup, a website that connects members who share similar interests, to plan rallies and meetings. To manage the logistics of using this tool, Dean staff were forced to establish regular meetings with online group organizers, creating the beginnings of online organizing infrastructure. Dean's campaign also frequented online forums to share talking points, generate new ideas, and solicit feedback. Dean was one of the earliest political candidates to use the web to fundraise, collecting more than $50 million over the course of his campaign. Unfortunately, Dean was unable to convert online infrastructure into actual votes. Despite his community's enthusiasm, the campaign faltered when it came to offline action due to a lack of ground support.

When it was time for the Obama camp to build their online grassroots movement, they made sure to learn from Dean's experiences. The Obama site's strategy could be summed up in one sentence: online organizing equals offline action. *"One of the lessons, obviously for us, is making sure that the grassroots enthusiasm translates into votes,"* Obama said in a *New York Times* interview. *"And that's something obviously that we're going to be paying a lot of attention to."*

Emergence of New Technologies: MoveOn.org and the 2006 Call for Change Campaign

Despite advances in online organizing strategy, Democrats didn't develop microtargeting capabilities until 2006, when organizations such as MoveOn fused data mining techniques with online phone-banking tools to challenge the Republican Party.

Founded in 1998 to involve people in the political process, MoveOn.org has grown into a national powerhouse with over four million members in February 2009. They have been pioneers in online grassroots strategy and were the first to tackle online phonebanking during the 2006 Congressional elections. *"We were facing a "turnout" rather than a persuasion election,"* they wrote in their 2006 report. They also recognized that successfully using this tool would significantly change the playing field in the approaching presidential elections.

They created the "liquid phonebank," named because voters could "pour in calls" from anywhere, allowing MoveOn members to collectively focus on a particular district no matter where they lived. The online tool guided callers to the district where their efforts were most needed, giving MoveOn the agility to quickly shift priorities as races unfolded and conditions changed. In addition, callers met once a week at a phone party, where they could socialize in person while using the online tools to make calls. This strengthened the sense of community, and helped connect people to the political issues. They combined Alex Gage's microtargeting techniques with Dean's people-powered online grassroots initiative and turned the tables on the GOP. Over the course of the congressional elections, over seven million calls would be made into sixty-one targeted districts using the online tool.

MOVEON.ORG

MoveOn.org was founded to petition government officials to censure President Bill Clinton and "move on," instead of impeaching him.

- 7,492 phone parties attended by 46,790 people
- 51,719 people used the online tools to make calls from their homes
- 7,001,102 total calls made using the online tool
- 61 districts targeted

This would lay the groundwork for the Obama team, who combined and refined online phonebanking, microtargeting, online organizing, and grassroots momentum to create the new model for modern campaigning.

The Innovation Context: The Political Landscape

In the race against the Clintons, the Obama team had developed a finely honed survival instinct that forced them to continuously reevaluate the playing field and identify new ways to connect with voters. This led to several key decisions that spurred innovative uses of social media and the creative application of online tools.

THE FIFTY-STATE STRATEGY

Traditionally, political parties tended to avoid engaging in states that were heavily controlled by their opponents. The Fifty-State Strategy, pioneered in 2004 by Democratic candidate Howard Dean, focused on building a presence for the party in all states, even ones where a victory was unlikely. The idea was to build increased awareness of Democrats who would be elected to local and state positions that would pave the way for future wins. The strategy was risky, since it would require people and financial resources in areas where their opponents had the advantage instead of concentrating on swing states where Democrats needed only a slightly higher number of popular votes to win. Obama was able to successfully execute the Fifty-State Strategy by ensuring that all online tools reinforced offline action and by empowering users to organize for his campaign in all states, including Republican strongholds.

TARGET THE MIDDLE

Unlike the Bush Administration's strategy of catering to voters who leaned to the right, the Obama team focused on the disaffected center. This allowed the campaign to open up a dialogue with independents as well as Republicans who were unhappy with the Bush Administration. From an online perspective, courting the center directed the tone and language of the blogs and the design of the website to ensure a welcoming and balanced atmosphere.

FOCUS ON SMALLER DONATIONS

The Obama camp also took note of Howard Dean's fundraising strategy, which raised $50 million over the course of his campaign, largely through small donations made online. Dean's average donation was $80. This was a sharp detour from the contemporary political strategy of tapping wealthy political donors to finance the campaign. In addition to generating free publicity for Dean, who started out as a "long-shot" candidate and became a front-runner, the technique was also less expensive than traditional telemarketing, direct mail, and hosted events. Finally, by soliciting small contributions the campaign was able to contact a donor multiple times, and donors were more likely to make multiple, small donations without exceeding the legal limit. Overall, John McCain was able to raise an impressive $360 million, but it seems paltry compared to the $750 million raised by the Obama campaign.

AT THE REPUBLIC NATIONAL CONVENTION IN SEPTEMBER 2008, vice-presidential nominee Governor Sarah Palin mocked Barack Obama's role as a community organizer. Members of Obama's online community demonstrated their displeasure by donating $10 million within the first twenty-four hours following Palin's speech. While substantial, this amount paled in comparison to Obama's fundraising total of $150 million for that month.

ONLINE FUNDRAISING

	OBAMA	**MCCAIN**
TOTAL AMOUNT RAISED	$750 MILLION	**$360 MILLION**
TOTAL AMOUNT RAISED ONLINE	$500 MILLION	**$75 MILLION**

PERSONAL EXPERIENCE

Welcome to Obama Land

My First Day at HQ

EN ROUTE TO CHICAGO

"I can't believe we're doing this," I said for the hundredth time. My boyfriend Jesse just grinned at me. It was well past midnight on a Thursday in June, and we were driving along a Michigan freeway en route to Chicago. I was to meet with Chris Hughes, Obama's Director of Internal Organizing the next morning. After corresponding a few times since his interview for *Grown Up Digital*, I realized that if I was really serious about wanting to work on the campaign I would have to meet with Chris in person. Knowing how swamped he was, I jumped at his first availability–30 minutes for a coffee on Friday afternoon.

Unfortunately, I was only able to confirm the date Thursday morning, which is how I found myself making the eight-hour drive at the last minute. We couldn't even spend the weekend in the Windy City because we were back for our friends' wedding on Saturday morning. Essentially, I was driving overnight for a half hour meeting that could very well lead to nothing. Or, it could be something.

We arrived in Chicago on Friday morning and spent a few hours exploring the Magnificent Mile. I made my way to Obama's campaign headquarters to meet Chris. Wearing jeans and a button up shirt, Chris was laid back, friendly, and funny. You would never guess that he was one of the co-founders of Facebook or the architect behind a revolutionary political social network. We walked to a nearby coffee shop where I tried my best to articulate why a geeky girl would want to participate in this election. In addition to having the opportunity of working with people like Chris, I found myself vocalizing a desire to participate in something big. *"I just want to be a part of it,"* I told him. He understood and would try to help. Even though he couldn't make any guarantees, I was ecstatic. All I could do now was cross my fingers and wait. Chris was true to his word and a few weeks later I connected with one of the staffers working on MyBO, Obama's social network. I received word that I could come down and become a full-time volunteer at Obama Headquarters!

Everything after that was a blur, as I raced to wrap up client projects and find a place to stay. I used Housingmaps.com, which displayed Craigslist rental listings on a Google map. I cross-referenced my top picks with Everyblock.com, a mash-up that listed all of the crimes in the vicinity to ensure I wasn't unwittingly relocating into a homicide hotzone. I contacted the three listings on my shortlist. I received a reply from Kevin, a journalism student who was looking for someone to sublet his bedroom for three months while he completed an internship in Washington, DC. Kevin lived with a college buddy named Sumair who worked from home writing technology reports. I made my decision when I found out that Sumair's company paid for high speed internet. Sold!

OUTSIDE OBAMA HQ ON MY VERY FIRST DAY

Jesse and I arrived in Chicago on Labor Day weekend, pulling up in front of a cheerfully painted blue house that was going to be my home for the next few months. The night before my first day, I tossed and turned, too excited to get a good night's rest. I kept jerking awake, thinking that I had slept through my alarm and missed my first day. Eventually, I gave up on sleep and got ready for work at 5:30 a.m. I arrived in downtown Chicago early, having said goodbye to Jesse, who was heading home to Toronto. I felt butterflies in my stomach as I rode up the elevators to the Campaign's National Office. What if I made a complete idiot of myself? The closest I had come to American politics was Seasons 1 and 2 of *The West Wing* that I had borrowed from a friend before making the trip down.

I was taken aback by the size of the operation. The campaign took up an entire floor of the building! I was greeted by Amy Hamblin and Emily Murphy, two members of the MyBO team I would be joining. Emily's bubbly personality and friendly smile quickly put me at ease as she gave me a tour of the office. New Media was housed in one corner and comprised of Internal Organizing (MyBO and N2N), External Organizing (Social Networks & Mobile), Video, Blogging, Email, Online Ads, Analytics, and Design. As I walked around the office, Obama's face looked back at me from posters, signs, and artwork that seemed to cover every possible surface. It was a little overwhelming and I wondered how it would feel to walk into a room and see my own face plastered on every wall.

OBAMA'S NAME WAS EVERYWHERE

New Media was a young department: most team members were dressed casually in jeans and Obama T-shirts, tightly clustered around desks and a few tables. It was loud and boisterous, and resembled a college dorm instead of a national political operation. I ended up securing a desk that was between Design, Organizing, and Video. It turned out to be an excellent vantage point to observe everything that was going on.

I was introduced to my new tablemate: the Obama Bot, a small robot that rolled around saying "Yes We Can" and "Fired up!" every time it encountered an object in its path. It was the creation of Jim Pugh, a member of the Analytics team who also happened to have a Ph.D in robotics. I made my first official contribution to both the Obama campaign and the field of micro-robotics by adding a printed picture of Obama's face to the top of the robot to give it a little character.

THE OBAMA BOT WAS MY TABLE MATE AND KEPT ME ENTERTAINED ON LONG DAYS

I had been familiarizing myself with MyBo's layout for a few hours when I noticed some of the staffers pushing chairs and desks out of the way and hauling in two large speakers. There was a sense of excitement in the air. *"Barack's calling in,"* one of the volunteers said to me, *"We better get a good seat before it's too late!"* I'm glad I paid attention, as the corner soon became crowded with staff and volunteers who perched themselves on nearby desks and leaned on walls. Someone dialed the conference lines and we heard field offices from across the country joining the call. There were 2,700 people listening in, including Campaign Manager David Plouffe. We all waited for Obama.

"Please hold for the senator," said a voice on the line and applause broke out in the room. Obama came on the line, *"How's everybody doing?"* He sounded upbeat but serious. *"I'm so proud of everything you've all accomplished but we have 60 more days to go,"* he said. *"So dig deep. It would be a great disappointment for us to fail after all this. They are going to come after us hard, and viciously, but I believe in you and I believe in this campaign. Let's get to work."*

What a first day.

TWO

THE CANDIDATE

CREATING A COMPELLING VISION

PERSONAL EXPERIENCE

The Race is On

Life in the trenches

Working on the campaign was an emotional roller-coaster. My entire universe became centered around the race between Barack Obama and John McCain. It was all I lived and breathed. I tracked new polls religiously and became addicted to The Huffington Post, TechPresident and FiveThirtyEight.com. I fluctuated between hopeful optimism and nerve-wracking despair.

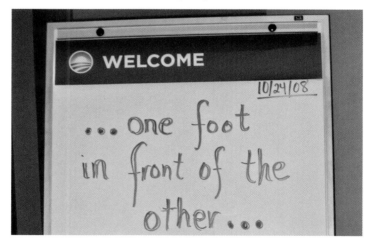

THIS SIGN OUTSIDE OF THE CAMPAIGN OFFICE WAS UPDATED DAILY

My days on the campaign were spent helping manage and maintain Barack's social network, MyBO. I moderated comments and approved groups. The job could be both tedious and incredibly amusing. As a volunteer, I was often sent to help anyone in New Media. This turned out to be an excellent opportunity to see how the various departments worked. I helped the mobile team process the thousands of SMS messages they received daily. I scoured MyBO for good examples of grassroots organizing and then passed the information on to the blog team. I evaluated websites for the online ads team and I reached out to some of my technology contacts as a part of social media outreach. No task was too small and I enjoyed every minute of it.

The energy and spirit of the new media team helped make the long campaign hours enjoyable. Someone was always ready with a smile or a funny YouTube video to share after a long day. Clickthru, our stuffed pink unicorn mascot, doubled as a pillow for anyone who needed to take a nap under a desk. The team bonded quickly and we often went out together on weekends and for late night drinks after work. I quickly learned about "Nubbing," New Media's method of sharing extra food. A "nub" was a small, half-moon addition attached to the end of a square desk. Any food left on a nub was considered up for grabs. Someone made a sign out of a paper plate and a ruler and its appearance caused a frenzy, as it meant the possibility of free food. At first, emails were sent out announcing "nubbed" goods, but it got to the point where the food would be gone by the time the email arrived in your inbox. Eventually, everyone developed a finely honed instinct where anytime you spotted a group of people heading toward a nub, you followed without asking questions, hoping it would lead to a delicious discovery.

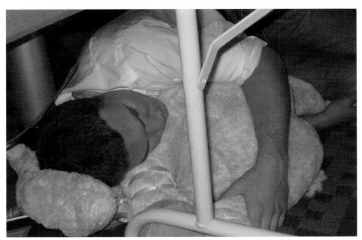

Zealan catching some shut eye on the ever faithful Clickthru

I loved watching the Presidential debates with the new media team. The campaign would order in mountains of food, including some of Chicago's famous deep dish pizza, and we would all huddle around the various televisions in the office. The team was a very funny bunch and they kept me laughing with their running commentary. Sometimes it felt as though we were watching our child play Little League. We fretted about how he was feeling, if he had gotten enough rest before the big game . Everyone would tense up when it was Barack's turn to answer a question. Murmurs of *"you can do it,"* and *"come on, Barack,"* could be heard from around the room. We applauded Barack's strong rebuttals and witty comments. Cries of *"yes, he totally nailed it!"* were common.

RAHAF AND CHRIS HUGHES, DIRECTOR OF ONLINE ORGANIZING.

A few days before the election, we had another conference call with Barack. *"I know we're doing well in the polls,"* he said. *"But I want you to forget all of that. I want you to remember New Hampshire. Nothing is guaranteed. So now is not the time to get cocky. Now is the time to double our efforts and work like we're twenty points behind. I know we can do this. The next time I speak with all of you, I want it to be as the next President of the United States,"* he finished to cheers.

David Plouffe then came on the line. *"We have the responsibility to elect Barack not because he would be a good president, but because he could be a great president,"* he said. *"This is one of those times you have the rare opportunity to walk alongside the giants of history and be a part of something bigger than yourself."* The campaign office was silent as every-one's attention was on Plouffe's next words. *"Let's finish this."*

I remember thinking that between the two of them, Obama and Plouffe made each person in the room feel as though they were personally responsible for winning the election. I know I walked back to my desk determined to give it my all. Before I knew it, it was November 4th, the day we had all been waiting for.

5 *The Birth of a Global Brand*

DESIGNING HOPE

THIS CHAPTER IS A CONVERSATION WITH SCOTT Thomas, the Obama campaign's design director, about Obama's branding and design process. Scott and I became friends while working on the campaign. We both shared a love of philosophy, design and newsanchor bloopers clips on YouTube. I was thrilled when he agreed not only to design this book, but also to answer some questions about his experiences creating and managing one of the world's most recognizable brands.

On Obama's branding and design situation when he joined the team

Like many political campaigns of the past, the Obama campaign was designing on the fly; time was the only design consideration. Of course every bad effect in the book was being used: drop shadows, beveled edges, elements that professional designers use in moderation. David Axelrod and his team did hire a designer, Sol Sender, in the early stages of the campaign to design the Obama "O" logo but all the various collateral was being designed by the campaign, which had yet to staff a full-time designer. John Slabyk and I began working for the campaign in September 2007. Initially tasked with having to design graphics for the New York City rally, we quickly realized that the days of having a "traditional" design process were over. We had to build an airplane while in flight.

On his first task on the job

We were tasked with a lot at once. Email landing pages, web graphics, rally signs, podium signs, and all these tasks had to be completed now. Triage became an important part of the job early on.

On the most challenging part

The most challenging part was not having the initial design process that we were used to; John and I really had to build backwards. The "mood boarding" process, the establishment of a visual language, the upfront designing was just impossible because of the speed at which we were moving. We were forced to build this process in time as we developed the brand's aesthetic.

On creating Obama's brand

At the onset, the campaign visuals were fairly inconsistent; stylistic considerations were based on a "design by committee" mentality—if one person asked for stars and stripes, stars and stripes was what they got. Everything was designed ad hoc, each element being on its own rather than as part of the cohesive whole. The campaign was using the typeface Gill Sans and many other disparate

typefaces to express their own particular concepts; for example, Women for Obama would use the script Zapfino, to express femininity. We realized this could quickly get out of hand and detract from the unity the campaign was trying to embody. Early on we decided to create a more consistent typographic palette, color palette, and overall consistent aesthetic. Under scrutiny, the typeface Gill Sans appeared elegant, sophisticated, and classic, but it also appeared stylistically formal, aloof, like a European black-tie affair.

So we began exploring other possibilities. We wanted the typeface to be versatile, bold, simple, elegant, and ideally to look historically

67

and stylistically American. The top choice became Gotham, a type-face designed in New York by Tobias Frere-Jones for *GQ* magazine. The face was inspired by the letters at the Port Authority Terminal in New York City; the type was "attractive but unassuming," and appeared blue collar but could dress up well. It was the perfect choice. Perfectly American.

We then began creating a more controlled and consistent color palette. The primary choice was blue, the color symbolizing the Democratic Party. We added a marbled gray similar to the pediment of the White House, and the accent or highlight color red, the color symbolizing the Republican Party, thus illustrating the underlying unity the campaign offered.

On revamping barackobama.com

The website redesign was launched in December 2007, right before the Iowa caucus, in preparation for the long battle that lay ahead. We spent the weeks and months before determining the site's main missions, considering our need for an efficient workflow, and con-structing the architecture of the new barackobama.com. The initial site design appeared cluttered, crowded, and busy; its growth was constantly stunted by "the fold." This term originally derived from the physical crease in a newspaper, the most important headlines being "above the fold." This idea was adopted by the web community, referring to the area of screen real estate visible without having to scroll. Barackobama.com was initially designed so that no content would appear below the fold. Imagine picking up a newspaper and unfolding it only to reveal nothing is below the crease. The new site design had to use the fold to our advantage, placing more important content toward the top of the page and creating a scrolling interface with organized information.

On creating distinctive brands for constituents that maintained an integrated branding feel

We decided early on that it would be great to design a logo mark for each constituency, while making it clear that each of them was part of a larger whole. This way groups of people could have a symbol that represented and expressed themselves and others like them. To keep the identity yet create a distinctive image.

Staying grounded in design

Scott reveals the true reason that Obama's logo and design work were so powerful consistency and a carefully cultivated brand message that effectively captured the spirit of hope, change, and action made the campaign's identity extremely powerful. Every time a voter interacted with a piece of the campaign's brand, whether it was a sign, button, or social network profile, they were greeted by familiar design elements that they recognized and identified with. This is an important reminder for organizations who get sidetracked by the flashier aspects of design: stay grounded in structure and attention to detail. Staying true to essence of the brand and protecting it from the whims of personal tastes is as important as choosing a color palette and font. The design team had to find the right balance between the chaotic nature of the campaign and the brand identity that would have to embody an agile and evolving movement.

SPOTLIGHT

Carly Pearlman,

GRAPHIC DESIGNER, OBAMA NEW MEDIA DESIGN TEAM

"The design team was extraordinary—exceptionally creative, unprecedentedly talented, and motivated beyond words. I truly felt like I was part of a family that not only inspired me to be the best designer that I could be, but was there to support me in whatever was needed, be it personal or campaign related. I woke up every morning feeling privileged and eager to be a part of my team. After the campaign ended it was the time spent with the design team that I missed the most. It was an honor to watch the world change with them by my side.

I think one of the most incredible things that I have learned from this experience, and that I hope this campaign has proven to be true, is that when you allow room for creativity and new ideas to thrive though often scary and never easy you can accomplish anything. Each and every one of us has the power to make change happen. Never lose sight of how important your individual contribution is to humanity and the lives of others. We rise and fall together, which is what makes life so magnificent and so very precious."

SPOTLIGHT

Jess Weida,
PRINT DESIGNER, OBAMA NEW MEDIA DESIGN TEAM

"In the days leading up to the election, the build-up was so difficult to process in real time. We couldn't even really talk about it, we all just knew. It just was. I felt hopeful but also very reluctant to assume anything about the outcome of the election. Of course I cared greatly about whether Barack would win, but I also was paying close attention to a lot of down-ticket races. I kept trying to anticipate what a loss would feel like and it was really, really difficult, though I had a hard time anticipating what a win would feel like too."

"My favorite moments were when I could really feel folks pulling together to make and contribute to something larger than themselves and when those seemingly small efforts made a significant difference. Those stories helped us get through and do what we did. One huge community effort!"

DESIGNING OBAMA'S SITE: LESSONS LEARNED

Site Architecture Tips

USER TESTING IS ESSENTIAL – The average company and the average budget do not usually encompass user testing, and it's one of the most effective tools you can use. When you build applications and websites for people without proper user testing you are doing them a disservice.

RELEASE EARLY, RELEASE OFTEN – Don't take too long to release the first version. Release it, see how it works, and iterate. Even if the product is not perfect, release early and release often. People appreciate improvement.

DOCUMENT PROCESSES TO CAPTURE ORGANIZATIONAL MEMORY – In a lot of organizations there is so much history they forget how long it took to get to the current state of affairs and the logic behind the decisions that were previously made.

— *Walker Hamilton, Site Architect, Obama New Media Design Team*

6 *My.BarackObama.com*

KEEP IT LOCAL, KEEP IT REAL

OBAMA'S OFFICIAL SOCIAL NETWORK, my.barackobama.com, was at the heart of the campaign's new media strategy. Affectionately referred to internally as MyBO, the site allowed users to create events, exchange information, raise funds, and connect with voters in their area. MyBO was the digital home base from which the campaign could mobilize its army of supporters. Creating an account required an email address and a password. Users didn't even have to confirm their email address. This was done to make the sign-up process as fast and easy as possible.

The drawback of this technique was that people could create accounts using fake email addresses with the sole intent of posting negative comments, a frequent occurrence requiring constant monitoring by the MyBO team. Online trolls, people who joined the community only to disrupt and insult members, were usually reported to online community managers within minutes and removed from the site. Over the course of the campaign, over three million people would create an account on MyBO and use the site's tools to organize for Obama.

Chris Hughes, Director of Online Organizing, was fascinated by the challenge of building a political social network. *"As great as Barack is, if the campaign hadn't been constituted in this idea of investing in our everyday supporters and helping them organize among themselves, I wouldn't have been as excited about the job,"* he said. One of Facebook's co-founders, Hughes left his role leading product development to join the campaign in Chicago. Armed with Facebook's community-building expertise, he applied the same principles to grow MyBO: Keep it real and keep it local. MyBO was built to strengthen existing connections with neighbors. Hughes understood that the primary function of MyBO was to enable supporters to reach each other and form their own connections. The MyBO team wanted to ensure that the online infrastructure would translate into an on-the-ground army that would help solicit votes.

Creating a sense of community was essential to MyBO's success, and campaign staff made a consistent effort to foster a supportive online atmosphere by providing plenty of resources to help users get the most out of the site. Videos offered a step-by-step tutorial on how to use each of the online tools, and a downloadable host guide helped organizers plan the perfect event from beginning to end. Campaign staff hosted weekly conference calls with MyBO members to exchange tips and insights about using the online tools. The team phoned hosts who had used MyBO to organize an event to offer support and advice. They often called back after the event as well, to make sure that everything had gone smoothly and to ask for feedback. This was one of the most rewarding parts of my own volunteer responsibilities. I loved connecting with real people and hearing the excitement in their voices when they heard that I was calling from National Headquarters to thank them for their efforts. *"We're fired up and ready to go,"* was an oft-repeated phrase. Their enthusiasm often buoyed my own spirits, especially when working twelve-hour days.

This chapter will look at the strategies that made MyBO an inviting and welcoming environment and some of the creative ways in which supporters used the site to organize for change.

Focus on what matters — We'll examine the way the profile, action center, and personal fundraising pages were used to keep the communities focused on the most important goal: getting Obama elected.

Incite the right actions — The campaign's activity index was refined to reward supporters who were using online tools to effectively organize offline.

Leverage creativity — The Obama team left enough flexibility in the events, group listings, and user blogs to give supporters an opportunity to create an intimate connection with the campaign through personal expression.

Focus on What Matters

The MyBO interface was carefully designed with usability in mind. The Obama team made sure it was easy for users to participate, raise funds, and stay updated with the campaign. Each MyBO account had the following components: dashboard, profile, action center, fundraising, network, and sidebar.

DASHBOARD

The dashboard was the user's homepage, a place to get an overview of all the action happening on MyBO. It provided easy shortcuts to quickly access the organizing tools, including personal fundraising and events. This kept the tools in sight—and foremost in the user's mind—whenever he or she logged on.

PROFILE

The profile allowed the user to upload a picture, create a user name, and state his or her location. Instead of listing favorite movies, TV shows, or music, a MyBO profile featured the answer two questions: *"Why do you support Barack Obama?"* and *"Are you registered to vote?"* The profiles allowed the user to customize content that was relevant to the mandate of the community: electing Obama.

ACTION CENTER

In August 2007, Chris Hughes introduced the MyBO action center on the official blog. *"What we must do now is channel all the enthusiasm and energy that you in this community have toward the completion of discrete goals that will help meet the campaign's objectives,"* he wrote. *"The Action Center is a place where you can go to find out exactly what the campaign needs from you today."*

Supporters were given a new task to complete every two weeks and encouraged to recruit new members from their circle of friends. Actions focused on priority items including voter registration drives, phonebank campaigns, and canvassing efforts.

FUNDRAISING

Each MyBO user could create a personal fundraising page, which included a thermometer graphic that tracked his or her progress. The page was customizable: users could articulate in their own words why supporting Barack was important to them. The personal fundraising page also came with a customized URL and embed code that could be placed in webpages and emails. This created a new way for the campaign to raise money because it didn't focus on supporting a candidate, but created an opportunity for friends and family

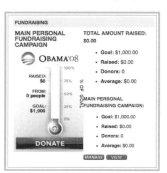

to support each other in order to reach personal fundraising goals. Instead of a stranger cold-calling to ask for a donation of five or ten dollars, it was your neighbor or friend who was raising money because she believed Barack would end the war in Iraq and bring her son back home. This made donating more personal and meaningful because in addition to supporting the campaign, your funds were providing a direct benefit to someone you know. Over the course of the campaign, 70,000 MyBO personal fundraising pages collected more than $35 million for the campaign.

NETWORK

MyBO users could exchange messages with each other much like an internal email account. The network feature allowed users to easily upload contacts from an Outlook or Gmail address book, encouraging members to invite their extended social network to join MyBO as well.

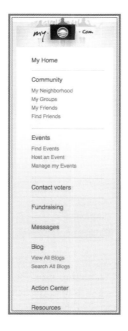

SIDEBAR

The sidebar was always visible, even when users navigated away from their dashboard to explore other areas of the Barack Obama site. This made sure that an online member's inbox, groups, and event information were always one click away.

Incite the Right Actions: The Activity Index

To keep supporters motivated and engaged, the Obama team had to make sure MyBO users felt they were making a difference in the campaign. Originally, MyBO contained a point system that assigned a value for various activities; a phone call was worth three points, making a donation was worth fifteen. A single cumulative score was calculated and displayed on a user's profile, reflecting their rank within the site. Members were ranked against each other and could lose their standing if another member accumulated more points. The idea was to mobilize voters by allowing them to directly measure their impact on the campaign through their organizing efforts. However, it quickly became evident to Chris Hughes, Director of Online Organizing, that certain people were trying to take advantage of the system. *"From the start, the emphasis was on quantifying an activist's contribution to the campaign, not on encouraging people to rack up points for the sake of racking up points,"* he wrote on the Obama official blog in August 2008. *"For some people, this wasn't always clear."* That same month, MyBO rolled out a simpler way for users to track their involvement, a feature called the activity index.

Instead of listing a score, the index clearly specified the types of activities a user engaged in: how many people they phoned, how many events they attended, and so on. The index rated the user's activity level on a scale of one to ten (one being least active, ten being most active), but there was a twist: it calculated the rating based only on recent activities.

This meant that users had to keep participating in order to maintain their rating. *"The more work you've done recently, the higher the number will be,"* Hughes explained on the Obama blog. This encouraged sustained behavior, ensuring a

---

KEEPING SCORE

15 POINTS for every event hosted

15 POINTS for a donation made to the personal fundraising page

10 POINTS for every door knocked on using the online canvassing tool

5 POINTS for every call made using the online call tool

3 POINTS for every event attended

3 POINTS for every blog post

3 POINTS for every group joined

---

continued stream of activity. In addition, the activity breakdown was publicly visible to other members in the community, further motivating people to participate. By placing more value on offline activities (hosting an event was worth fifteen points compared to three points for joining a group), the campaign also acted on its strategy of "offline action," rewarding people for mobilizing in the real world.

The index became an accurate and efficient way of segmenting the community based on activity level. Users who achieved a certain rating out of ten were given access to special resources, such as training videos on how to maximize the use of the online tools. It also helped state field organizers spot highly motivated users in their area who could be recruited to join the campaign in a more formal capacity, such as becoming a neighborhood leader or phonebank organizer. It made it easy to identify supporters who were more willing to engage with the campaign, without excluding those who wanted to get involved on a lesser scale. Membership became a continuum on which every supporter could find his or her own sweet spot. The index was also applied to entire groups, so that anyone could see how active an entire membership was at a glance.

Leverage Creativity

GROUPS

MyBO groups allowed users to quickly and easily connect with other voters who shared similar interests. Groups ranged from people with the same occupations (Electricians for Obama), to location (Texas for Obama), to demographics (Women for Obama). Groups were given their own homepage, complete with a blog, directory, electronic mailing list, a collective activity index, and a group fundraising meter. By the end of the campaign over 35,000 groups were created by volunteers.

Not all groups were focused solely on fundraising or organizing; some were used as a way to send a message to the Obama campaign. The most notable of these was one of the largest MyBO groups, made up of members who opposed the senator's stance on an amendment to the Foreign Intelligence Surveillance Act (FISA). The bill would grant the president more leeway to spy on citizens' private communications and would grant immunity to telephone companies who were accused of illegal surveillance. Obama had originally stated that he opposed modernizing FISA. In June 2008, he released a statement saying that he would support the FISA Amendments Act of 2008 being considered by the House of Representatives, but that he would try to remove the retroactive legal immunity part before it came to the Senate floor. A few months later he changed his stance and supported the modernization of the bill, including the retroactive legal immunity.

His support of the bill angered many community members on MyBO and a group was formed in June 2008 called *"Senator Obama, Please Vote NO on Telecom Immunity—Get FISA Right."* It grew to several thousand people and quickly became one of the largest groups on MyBO. Many speculated about what the official response would be, if any, and how the senator's progressive campaign would respond to voices of dissent within their own community.

On July 3, 2008, New Media Director Joe Rospars posted an official response from Obama on the site's official blog. In a demonstration of the site's effectiveness in getting Obama's attention, an official statement was released addressed directly to those who had taken issue with his stance. Obama took the time to explain the reasoning behind his position and acknowledged the impact of the MyBO community, saying, *"Now, I understand why some of you feel differently about the current bill, and I'm happy to take my lumps on this site and elsewhere. For the truth is that your organizing, your activism and your passion is an important reason why this bill is better than previous versions."* He wrote, *"No tool has been more important in focusing peoples' attention on the abuses of executive power in this Administration than the active and sustained engagement of American citizens. That holds true not just on wiretapping, but on a range of issues where Washington has let the American people down."*

Obama set the tone for future communications and interactions with community members saying, *"I cannot promise to agree with you on every issue. But I do promise to listen to your concerns, take them seriously, and seek to earn your ongoing support to change the country."* He also outlined what he intended regarding FISA if he was elected, promising to have his attorney general *"conduct a comprehensive review of all our surveillance programs, and to make further recommendations on any steps needed to preserve civil liberties and to prevent executive branch abuse in the future."* Once again, his actions reaffirmed the campaign's message of hope and change, while maintaining transparency about why he was voting for the bill.

The new media team took an extra step. Joe Rospars announced that for thirty minutes following the post, three members of the policy team would be monitoring the comment sections to respond to any questions or concerns that readers might have. Deputy National Policy Director Danielle Gray, Senior Foreign Policy Advisor Denis McDonough, and Foreign Policy Advisor and Senior Speechwriter Ben Rhodes spent ninety minutes wading through over six hundred comments and participating in a dialogue with concerned supporters. The campaign made it clear that they were both listening to their supporters and willing to talk with them regarding any feedback they might have. This also shifted the conversation from complaining or protesting to constructively discussing the issue and learning about Obama's reasons for voting the way that he did. Supporters who participated would then share this information with other members of the community who might have similar concerns.

SENATOR OBAMA, PLEASE VOTE NO ON TELECOM IMMUNITY- GET FISA RIGHT

23,211 members
4,919 Events hosted
35,744 Events attended
215,090 Calls made
5,263 Doors knocked
94,826 Blog posts
$726,977.32 Raised

FLORIDA WOMEN FOR OBAMA CAMPAIGN FOR CHANGE

39,102 members
4,831 Events hosted
37,180 Events attended
127,874 Calls made
12,549 Doors knocked
42,364 Blog posts
$349,885.30 Raised

MACS FOR BARACK

314 members
1,740 events hosted
6,690 events attended
17,723 calls made
681 doors knocked
28,004 blog posts
$236,290.87 raised

ENVIRONMENTALISTS FOR OBAMA

36,285 members
14,953 Events hosted
92,338 Events attended
740,731 Calls made
12,610 Doors knocked
162,897 Blog posts
$2,066,717.54 Raised

AUDACITY OF HOPE
BOOK DONATIONS FOR OBAMA
161 members
2,012 Events hosted
8,667 Events attended
16,042 Calls made
373 Doors knocked
30,634 Blog posts
$58,127.06 Raised

POSTCARDS FOR OBAMA
(POSTCARDS FOR VOTES)
124 members
530 Events hosted
3,200 Events attended
17,251 Calls made
415 Doors knocked
4,965 Blog posts
$40,196.79 Raised

STUDENTS FOR BARACK OBAMA
36,719 members
19,635 Events hosted
79,161 Events attended
405,629 Calls made
4,531 Doors knocked
174,259 Blog posts
$1,737,475.70 Raised

EVENTS

The real spirit of the community could be seen in the more than 200,000 offline events organized through MyBO. The events feature gave community members a way to incorporate the qualities that Obama represented into their daily lives and to inject a personal touch to the campaign. In addition to traditional events such as phonebanks or neighborhood canvassing, MyBO members invented thousands of other creative ways to express their support. Events included everything from dinner parties and themed biking tours to art and fashion shows, comedy nights, and local movie premiers. The community's actions embodied the Obama brand in a way that transcended marketing and public relations initiatives.

In January 2008, two Yale University students launched a venture called Obama Works. In a column in the *Yale Daily News*, Justin Kosslyn and David Manners-Weber asked, *"What if a portion of the grassroots campaign were dedicated to visible public service projects?"* In other words, how could MyBO users demonstrate through actions the values of the Obama brand within communities across America? Their answer: organized community service where Obama support- ers could do good while taking part in events that represented the campaign's values. The activities would have to be simple enough to be easily implemented anywhere. They suggested three types of events: Neighborhood cleanups, charity runs, and various small- scale local projects. *"Residents driving through town squares and walking through local parks would find groups of enthusiastic Obama volunteers picking up cigarette butts and candy wrappers,"* they wrote. They also suggested a five-kilometer charity run to support local families and projects ranging from *"re-tiling the bathroom in a local women's shelter to distributing children's books from the local book bank."*

The goal was to rebuild the American public's trust in politicians through reputation and a track record of civic service and to dem- onstrate that through grassroots organizing, big changes can take place. Kosslyn and Manners-Weber called their community service acts "Obama Works." News of their work quickly spread on MyBO and soon supporters in other areas started organizing their own events. Local chapters were soon established across the country. The Minneapolis chapter boasted over forty members who organized clean-ups of local parks and streets. The story was picked up by the media, giving excellent press coverage to the campaign.

BarackFest (Breakfast)

Since March 2007, Dan of Ft. Collins, Colorado, has been using the power of breakfast to bring people together. During the campaign, on the first Sunday of the month he served fresh omelets, crepes, stratas, and pancakes to supporters who gathered to trade campaign experiences and personal stories. Each event raised between $200 and $500.

Barack Birthday Bashes

In Montara, California, eighty people gathered to celebrate Barack's birthday. Festivities included a birthday cake, a huge cardboard cutout for photos, a large birthday card, and a list of forty-seven reasons to vote for Senator Obama. They also screened A&E's Biography channel episode on Barack Obama. After the fun, party-goers recruited local volunteers and canvassed Spanish-speaking voters in New Mexico.

Soul Line Dancers

Over 60 dancers wearing "Soul Line Dancers for Obama" shirts busted out their best dance moves on the streets of Oakland, California. Many residents out for a stroll past the Lake Merritt Columns joined in the fun. The group also set up a table for donations and new voter registrations.

Basement Bhangra

South Asians for Obama in co-operation with Obama NYC, Latinos for Obama, Asian Americans for Obama, Queens County for Obama, and Generation Obama sponsored "Basement Bhangra," an Indian dance party that educated voters about Obama's positions on various key issues. Over 400 people showed up for the event in New York City and danced the night away.

USER BLOGS

Each MyBO account included a blog where supporters could post about their experiences and thoughts throughout the race. The blogs were a great way to share information and personal stories, and helped connect Obama supporters to each other. It gave supporters like Maria from Missoula, Montana, a platform to have their voices heard. Maria had become an Obama supporter in 2005, after stumbling on a keynote made by the senator to Citizens United for Research in Epilepsy (CURE). Having recently lost her daughter to the medical condition, she used her MyBO blog in early 2007 to express how Obama's words had *"comforted me during a most painful time in my life."*

Maria had already knocked on doors and made phone calls on behalf of Barack but she wanted to do more. She came up with an innovative idea that combined her love of food with her belief in hope, change, and action. She spent the month of April 2008 connecting with Obama supporters on MyBO and compiling 160 stories and recipes, which she assembled into an online cookbook. She posted the entire collection on her MyBO blog and called it "The Obama Family Cookbook," as a reflection of the camaraderie and friendship that was felt on the site. Anyone could access the content for free, but Maria asked voters to donate what they could. She raised $2,000 through online donations but didn't stop there.

"This is a real grassroots cookbook, like the old-fashioned-but-fun church and school cookbooks of yore," she posted on her blog. She collected recipes from all fifty states, as well as England, the Virgin Islands, and the Netherlands. The cookbook would be a great keepsake of *"the experience we've had in creating our Obama family."* The cookbook is dedicated to her daughter, Carrie.

I asked Maria about her experiences with the campaign. *"I was a part of the campaign—as were millions of others just like me,"* she said. *"I had never worked on a political campaign or donated any money to one. I felt that it was my campaign, our campaign, and that I was (and still am) working for the common good. I felt 'empowered' for the first time in my life."* Obama's message of being our brother's keeper resonated with her. *"That is the kind of world I want for my children."*

SWEET POTATO PIE RECIPE
Submitted by Carla B from Waldorf, Maryland

My name is Carla and I received this recipe from a single Air Force active duty member about 19 years ago. I have been married to an Air Force member for almost 20 years. I would often host a dinner at our home for active duty members who had no place to have Thanksgiving dinner. The troops didn't have to bring anything but themselves for dinner, but one troop brought sweet potato pies with him and they were the BEST sweet potato pies I've ever had. I begged him for the recipe and about two weeks later he brought the recipe. I must say that I've served the best sweet potato pie for Thanksgiving dinners ever since. I get kudos every year from Thanksgiving dinner guests and many of them have requested the recipe. This recipe is even more special to me now because the Air Force member who gave me this recipe 19 years ago, died while serving in Iraq two years ago, leaving behind a wife and two beautiful children. This sweet potato pie Ba-racks!

1 8″ frozen piecrust or 1 Pillsbury ready-made rolled refrigerated piecrust
1 medium sweet potato (boiled with skin on until done)
1/2 cup of granulated sugar
1/2 stick of butter (softened)
1/2 tsp. of pure vanilla flavoring
1/2 tsp. of lemon flavoring
1/2 tsp. of orange flavoring
1/2 tsp. of maple flavoring
1/2 tsp. of butter flavoring
1/4 tsp. of nutmeg
1/4 tsp. of cinnamon
1/8 tsp. of cream of tartar
1/2 cup Carnation evaporated canned milk or 1/2 cup of Borden's sweetened condensed milk
1 tbs. flour
1 egg

Peel boiled sweet potato and place in mixing bowl. Add sugar, softened butter to bowl and mix together with sweet potato. Add vanilla, lemon, orange, maple, and butter flavorings. Mix slightly. Add cream of tartar, flour, cinnamon, nutmeg, and milk, and mix together. If mix is too thick, you can add a little more milk; if mix is too thin, you can add a little more flour. Once mixed together, you can taste test and add any additional flavoring you desire. In a separate bowl, beat egg and add to mix and mix it all together. Add mix to piecrust and bake in an oven at 350 degrees for one hour. Remove pie from oven and let cool. Serve with whipped cream and enjoy! Yields one 8-inch pie, approximately 6 servings.

SOCIAL MEDIA LESSONS

FOCUS ON WHAT MATTERS — Within MyBO, the mandate was very clear: use the online tools to organize offline action. From the profile that asked you to describe why you supported Obama to the action center that directed users to areas of priority, offline action was constantly reinforced. When building an online community it is often helpful to spell out in a few lines what the goals and mandates are. Is the mandate clear? Does it make sense? More importantly, does it resonate with what your members are already trying to do? If you answered "no" to any of the above questions, then it's probably a good idea to step back and refine the purpose of your community. Establishing the mandate is only part one of this exercise. The second part involves making sure that all of the features and activities of the community reinforce the mandate. Examine everything from the interface and design to the ways that you envision member interaction. Be sure everything is designed to push your mandate forward.

INCITE THE RIGHT ACTIONS — Building incentives that reward the right type of action is an important part of community building. The activity index helped reward those who were organizing offline by assigning a higher point value to offline activities. It also encouraged frequent and continual support by factoring in the frequency of activities in the algorithm. This ensured that members of the community were not only going out and organizing for Obama, but that they were doing so on a regular basis.

LEVERAGE CREATIVITY — The events, group listings, and user blogs allowed supporters to engage with the campaign on their own terms. Successful communities are flexible and allow members to express themselves and have a role in shaping the community. Thanks to the creativity of users, new event categories and groups were formed in an innovative way without straying from the community's mandate.

7 *Neighbor to Neighbor*

THE TALKS THAT MATTER

There are many ways for you to have an impact on this campaign, but the single most important thing you can do is to talk directly to voters. There's nothing more powerful and effective than everyday people reaching out to their neighbors—or people in a neighboring battleground state—and talking about why they support Barack. (Barack Obama HQ Blog)

Neighbor to Neighbor (N2N) was Obama's online phonebanking tool that allowed supporters to make calls on behalf of the campaign from the comfort of their own home. It was launched in September 2007 as a way to help supporters reach out to undecided voters, recruit volunteers, and quickly share information. Accessed through a user's MyBO account, N2N added all calls made by a user into his or her activity index.

Voters who wanted to participate in N2N could choose to take part in a phone campaign or a door-to-door canvassing campaign. Phone campaigns targeted specific constituencies (Women for Obama), states (Ohio for Obama), or specific goals (Recruit Volunteers). The Obama team listed the different phone campaigns in order of priority so users would know which ones needed the most immediate support. Phone campaigns also took into account a user's location to avoid problematic situations such as having California supporters phone voters in Ohio too late in the evening because of the time difference between the states.

Canvassing campaigns used a supporter's zip code to produce a list of independent voters in the neighborhood to reach out to. The list came complete with a printable map showing volunteers exactly where to go. Scripts were available for printing out along with a record sheet to keep track of visits. Users reported their results through N2N when they were finished and that data was also shared with the local field office.

Once a campaign was selected and the user was ready to begin, they received a list of people to contact. An interactive script was provided to guide the conversation and enabled the user to record

the caller's answers in real time. Once the call was completed, results were submitted to the N2N system. The data was then sent directly to field organizers who could follow up on the ground. Effectively, it transformed every home computer into a fully functioning field office.

The success of Neighbor to Neighbor was dependent on two things:

MAKING USERS FEEL COMFORTABLE — The Obama team put supporters at ease by providing a multitude of ways for them to use N2N, including varying the type of calls and the amount of training.

CREATING SMALL AND FREQUENT CAMPAIGNS — The campaign also focused on a variety of campaigns that aimed to fulfill different goals. This kept things interesting and increased the likelihood that supporters would participate in more than one campaign. This also attracted first-time users who would be drawn to a particular calling campaign that they could relate to personally.

Making Users Feel Comfortable

N2N offered a variety of calling and canvassing campaigns, making it easier for supporters to pick and choose how they wanted to engage. Some people were perfectly comfortable dialing up independents and persuading them to vote for Obama, while others cringed at the thought and preferred to call Obama supporters who would be more open to volunteering with the campaign. There were supporters who loved making phone calls and others who preferred speaking with their neighbors face to face. The campaign provided a variety of way for supporters to get involved, giving them the opportunity to pick a method of participation that they were most comfortable with.

Some supporters signed up for N2N and immediately started making calls, while others needed a little more encouragement before they were ready to pick up the phone or knock on a door by themselves. The campaign understood that for supporters to feel comfortable with the tool, they had to learn how to use it properly use it. The National Call Team was created to encourage N2N users to use the tool regularly. During a weekly conference call, senior campaign staffers, seasoned N2N users, and N2N novices came together to exchange tips and ideas about how best to leverage N2N.

Eventually, this feature evolved into state-specific call teams that connected individual N2N users with others in their area to foster an atmosphere of community. The Colorado Call Team invited supporters to participate in a conference call with Obama Colorado State Director Ray Rivera, Senator Ken Salazar, Senator Amy Klobuchar, and former Colorado Governor Roy Romer to discuss the importance of calling voters in battleground states. *"I know Colorado real well. We can win this state,"* said Romer. *"Your help is critical; Colorado could be the difference in this election."* A recording of the call was placed on the Obama website so other supporters could listen, get inspired, and sign up for a calling campaign in their area.

During my time at the campaign, I learned of volunteers who were making upwards of one thousand calls from their homes each week. This was even more remarkable considering that anything over one hundred calls is considered extraordinary. One woman named Jane Whitington from West Virginia used N2N to make over nine hundred calls recruiting potential Obama volunteers. She was profiled on the official Obama blog for her efforts. *"It's been wonderful. I've met so many interesting people,"* she was quoted as saying. *"And you know at first I was doing so much calling, I felt a little bad, like it would ruin team morale if I was calling more than everyone else. But then I thought, nah."*

By providing a variety of ways to engage and ensuring that supporters understood how N2N worked, the campaign helped the online community feel comfortable, empowered, and capable of using the tool to organize for Obama.

Creating Small and Frequent Campaigns

MyBO supporters were encouraged to get involved with N2N through the introduction of frequent calling and canvassing campaigns that encompassed a wide variety of topics and goals. The campaigns would only last for a few days and the entire new media platform would promote the campaign, cheering callers on, until it was finished. This helped keep the tool fresh, as there was always a new type of calling campaign going on. This approach also increased the potential user base because the various campaigns appealed to a variety of people.

Voter lists assigned to a particular MyBO user expired after three days. This ensured that if a volunteer was unable to complete all the calls they had signed up for, the names would be returned to the pool and assigned to another caller. This took the pressure off N2N volunteers and encouraged them to set high call goals because they knew that another supporter could step in and finish the job if they couldn't.

GOAL-SPECIFIC CAMPAIGNS

A common type of calling campaign was to set a particular number of phone calls as a goal and to challenge N2N users to meet it. For example, just after Obama's Maine victory, the Obama team challenged the online community to make 40,000 phone calls in one day, and they did.

PEER-TO-PEER CAMPAIGNS

Peer-to-peer campaigns invited members of particular constituencies to talk to each other about Barack Obama. For example, on Women's Day in 2008, the campaign launched a one-day calling campaign inviting women to reach out to each other and discuss the campaign issues that matter to them. Speaking with voters they could relate to helped break down barriers associated with calling a stranger on the phone. Sharing common ground resulted in callers who were generally more knowledgeable about the issues that could sway a potential voter.

ISSUE-SPECIFIC CAMPAIGNS

The campaign enlisted supporters to use the online phonebanking tool to reach out and discuss a particular topic. The Turn the Page in Iraq campaign invited supporters to knock on doors and talk to their neighbors about Obama's exit strategy for the war in Iraq. Supporters then used MyBO to create their own canvassing events.

VOLUNTEER RECRUITING CAMPAIGNS

Supporters were often asked to reach out and enlist more volunteers for the campaign. Callers used N2N to recruit volunteers who could help out in a variety of ways, either through phonebanking and canvassing or by donating their time to help set up a rally or event.

INFORMATIONAL CAMPAIGNS

Informational campaigns let voters know about upcoming events that might be of interest. For example, N2N users contacted Obama supporters across the country to let them know about Obama's prime-time television special, and encouraged them to host watch parties or fundraising events.

GET OUT THE VOTE CAMPAIGNS

Supporters also used N2N for calling campaigns aimed at getting out the vote. Volunteers called voters not only to encourage them to go to the polls, but also to provide polling location hours, explain what information they needed to bring, and offer advice about what to do if they ran into problems. The calling campaign was taken up by volunteers in non-battleground states; calls into battleground state Ohio, for example, came in from New York and Michigan. This freed up supporters in battleground states to knock on doors and participate in more on-the-ground efforts. N2N allowed the campaign to focus nationwide attention on a particular part of the country that needed attention both instantly and effortlessly.

SOCIAL MEDIA LESSONS

MAKING USERS COMFORTABLE — The Obama team had a high success rate with N2N campaigns that used peer-to-peer contacts. For example, students would call other students, Latino voters would speak to other Latino voters, and so on. It turned the impersonal act of cold-calling a stranger into a conversation structured around common ground. This put N2N users at ease, and made them warmer and more effective Obama supporters.

When asking your online community to complete a particular task, identify ways you can make their experience more comfortable. Do they need more training, such as a video tutorial? Do they have a choice in customizing how they engage? Do they feel supported if they run into an issue? Putting some thought into setting online community members at ease will ensure a higher rate of participation, and will usually lead to higher-quality content.

CREATING SMALL AND FREQUENT CAMPAIGNS — The strategy of creating small but frequent initiatives played a big part in the success of N2N. It allowed the Obama team to break up a two-year campaign into smaller, more manageable chunks. Smaller campaigns allowed the campaign to reach tangible goals and gave participants the opportunity to celebrate successes. The diversity of calling campaigns kept users engaged. A campaign targeting Maine voters was much different than Turn the Page in Iraq, which in turn differed from women calling women for Obama. Despite using the same tool, each campaign had a different focus, goal, and target audience. This allowed community members to engage in causes that they felt passionately about instead of forcing them to stick to one static script for the entire campaign. Some supporters enjoyed the thrill of helping the campaign achieve a certain number of calls in one day, while others gravitated toward campaigns where they talked to people like them about things they cared about.

Ask people to participate in different and creative ways. If you are soliciting feedback, invite users to submit their responses in different ways, such as a video, photo, or written comment. Try to always include a fresh perspective and provide new ways for your readers to engage with your content.

Ryan Hoffman,
ONLINE ORGANIZING TEAM INTERN

JOINED THE CAMPAIGN: July 14, 2008

ROLE: "I worked mostly as an administrator and moderator on My.BarackObama.com, but I also did work related to the texting team. Also, under Mary Joyce [Director of New Media Operations], I was the head supervisor of the largest mass mailing in the campaign's history, the one that sent out 13,000 packets to convention watch parties held across the nation for Obama's nomination acceptance speech in Denver."

ON THE ONLINE ORGANIZING TEAM: "Everyone kept going back and forth between feeling very positive and very anxious. Overall though, we were hard workers and were much more in our element when working long hours and late at night. 'Workaholic' is another good way to describe people."

ON ELECTION NIGHT: "I was very anxious, honestly, for the first time in the entire campaign! I had always been weirdly positive that we were going to win the thing even during the worst polling period of the year, immediately after Palin was nominated. It wasn't until Pennsylvania was called that I started feeling good though, and Ohio when I started celebrating because I knew we had won it."

ON COMING IN TO WORK ON NOVEMBER 5, 2008: "Very, very, very odd. Workload dropped off significantly, and for the first time I became worried about what the heck I was going to do for a living now that the job was done. Besides that though, very proud and relieved about our historic win."

ON FAVORITE CAMPAIGN MOMENTS: "Obama's nomination address at the DNC in Denver and the night Senator Biden came into the office to talk to us."

RYAN'S MESSAGE: "Keep it up, America. We did a great thing, but the real work remains ahead of us. Stay positive, be willing to sacrifice for the greater good, and always, always hold your elected officials accountable for their actions and never fall for the cheap old tricks that have gotten so many candidates elected in the first place."

8 *Email*

A MESSAGE WRITTEN JUST FOR YOU

EMAIL WAS THE MOST COMMON WAY PEOPLE CONNECTED with the campaign. Supporters became familiar with seeing messages from various staffers in their inboxes and could follow the campaign through a variety of perspectives: a strategic bird's-eye view from Plouffe, frontline reports from Carson, and messages of hope and change from Barack himself. Subscribers would also receive emails from Michelle Obama, Joe Biden, Jill Biden, and even Al Gore encouraging them to get involved in the movement. To nurture these relationships, all campaign emails embodied a three-word mantra: respect, empower, and include.

Emails from Barack Obama were drafted by Stephen Geer and his team, which marked another difference from traditional political campaigns where any copy from the candidate is drafted by speechwriters. This was the first campaign where email was considered on equal footing with other communication mediums. The Obama team used email as an integral platform to engage supporters, bloggers, and online media. Often overlooked by traditional communications departments, email has one major advantage: speed. According to Geer, some emails went *"right from Obama's mouth into an email,"* making the campaign more agile and current when connecting with supporters.

> *"Respect, empower, and include was the heart of online and offline grassroots mobilization."*
> — *Stephen Geer, Obama's Director of Email and Online Fundraising*

Growing the email list was a constant priority. *"We had a great response to simple incentives—free stuff like bumper stickers,"* Geer said. Obama rallies drastically increased email list membership by providing an excellent opportunity to tap into the excitement of the moment and ask supporters to sign up for updates. By the time the election rolled around, the Obama team had collected over 13 million email addresses, compared with John Kerry's 3 million names in 2004.

McCain's camp was heavily criticized for the lack of apparent strategy in their email. Patrick Ruffini, a blogger from the popular political and technology blog techPresident, described McCain's emails as *"Tolstoy in my inbox,"* referring to the text heavy, image-free messages that were sometimes as long as five hundred words with only one hyperlink. McCain also seemed to miss the opportunity to open a more informal dialogue with voters. The McCain campaign's email tended to be quite formal in tone and closely resembled press releases or authorized statements.

In contrast, emails from the Obama campaign often used content from Barack's eloquent speeches and reflected the way he would speak. Each message was crafted to be the perfect mix of text, pictures, and hyperlinks. Emphasis was placed on brevity: concise paragraphs that quickly got to the point. Since the emails were crafted specifically for the medium, the Obama team's email had a much more intimate tone.

The Obama email team's mandate was four-fold:

MOBILIZATION — Ensure a consistent messaging strategy that encompassed both short - and long-term communication objectives.

MESSAGING — Reinforce the campaign's overall new media strategy to encourage offline action.

MOTIVATION — Draft compelling content that would invite voters to contribute financially to the campaign.

MEANINGFUL CONTENT — Provide supporters with meaningful and relevant content that was applicable to their personal situation.

From: Al Gore
Subject: **Elections Matter**
Date: November 2, 2008

In 2000, the entire election came down to a small number of votes in one county in Florida. Four years later, we came up short by an average of nine voters per precinct in Ohio. A small change in voter turnout would have made

all the difference. Take it from me, elections matter. And this time, supporters like you can make it happen. I know this might not be possible for everyone, but I'm asking you to consider volunteering anytime between now and Election Day—Tuesday, November 4. With so much at stake this year, we can't miss any opportunity to get more voters to the polls—and make sure their votes are counted. You have an important role to play in this election. Please sign up to volunteer.

Mobilization: Escalating Involvement Strategy

Stephen Geer describes the email team's approach to voter engagement as an *"escalating involvement strategy that was metered out and had triggered frequency."* This meant that Obama emails asked supporters to do a little bit more each time they participated in the campaign. If a supporter signed up to attend a local neighborhood event, they were invited to volunteer. If a supporter volunteered, they were asked to host a phonebank or fundraising drive at their home. The campaign offered an array of increased responsibilities to those who were eager to get involved. By up-selling campaign involvement, regular volunteers were transformed into full-fledged organizers and community leaders who became the heart of the Obama grassroots movement.

The emphasis was on clearly stating what needed to be done. Whether it was knocking on doors, calling voters, or donating money, *"the ask"* was always simple, clear, and concise. On September 4, 2008, John McCain announced that Alaska Governor Sarah Palin would be his running mate. At the Republican National Convention, Palin mocked Obama's experience as a community organizer. *"I guess a small-town mayor is sort of like a community organizer, except that you have actual responsibilities,"* she said to a cheering crown in St. Paul, Minnesota. Mere hours later, the email team had crafted a response from Campaign Manager David Plouffe intended to mobilize the very people Palin had insulted. *"They insulted the very idea that ordinary people have a role to play in our political process,"* Plouffe wrote. *"Let's clarify something for them right now. Community organizing is how ordinary people respond to out-of-touch politicians and their failed policies."* Governor Palin had unwittingly tapped into the narrative of empowerment that the email team had been building all along. Plouffe's email likened Palin's disdain for community organizers to an attack on every single Obama volunteer who believed they could make a difference. Obama supporters responded by contributing $10 million in the first twenty-four hours, making September 4, the single biggest day of fundraising in political history. This type of open dialogue mixed with calls to action cemented a strong and positive working relationship between supporters and the campaign. *"It gave people a sense of ownership over the whole process,"* Geer explained.

From: David Plouffe
Subject: **Last Minute Attacks**
Date: September 3, 2008
(THE DAY BEFORE MCCAIN'S SPEECH AT THE REPUBLICAN NATIONAL CONVENTION)

In the next 36 hours, the McCain campaign will be pouring millions of dollars—if not tens of millions—into negative attack ads against Barack Obama. Before John McCain accepts the Republican nomination on Thursday, his campaign has to spend every last dollar of primary funds they've raked in from Washington lobbyists and special interest PACs. With so much at stake, we can't allow another election to be determined by petty and divisive political tactics. Please make your donation today. I know we've asked a lot from supporters like you recently, and many of you contributed just last week. But the stakes are high, and there are less than 9 weeks before Election Day. It's going to require unprecedented resources to defeat John McCain and bring about the change America so desperately needs. Thank you for all you do.

From: David Plouffe
Subject: **What You Just Saw**
Date: September 4, 2008
(THE FINAL DAY OF THE REPUBLICAN NATIONAL CONVENTION)

I wasn't planning on sending you something tonight. But if you saw what I saw from the Republican convention, you know that it demands a response. I saw John McCain's attack squad of negative, cynical politicians. They lied about Barack Obama and Joe Biden, and they attacked you for being a part of this campaign. But worst of all—and this deserves to be noted—they insulted the very idea that ordinary people have a role to play in our political process. You know that despite what John McCain and his attack squad say, everyday people have the power to build something extraordinary when we come together. Will you make a donation right now to remind them?

From: Joe Biden
Subject: **McCain's Speech**
Date: September 5, 2008
(THE DAY AFTER THE REPUBLICAN NATIONAL CONVENTION)

John McCain just accepted the Republican nomination and adopted the most conservative platform in the history of his party. After days of negative attacks—and no mention of real proposals to fix our economy, get more people healthcare, or make America safer—the party that brought you eight years of disastrous policies is asking for four more. Well, not if we have anything to say about it. Across this nation, people like you have joined this movement because you believe that we are better than the past eight years. And now that we are entering the final stretch, it's going to take all of us to bring the change we need. Will you make a donation at this crucial moment to change our country?

From: Barack Obama
Subject: **The Attacks**
Date: September 5, 2008
(THE DAY AFTER THE REPUBLICAN NATIONAL CONVENTION)

Why would the Republicans spend a whole night of their convention attacking ordinary people? With the nation watching, the Republicans mocked, dismissed, and actually laughed out loud at Americans who engage in community service and organizing. Our convention was different. We gave the stage to everyday Americans who hunger for change and stepped up to make phone calls, knock on doors, and raise money in small amounts in their communities. You may have missed it, but we also showed the country a video with the faces and voices of those organizers, volunteers, and donors from every corner of the country. Watch the video and make a donation now to show that in this election, ordinary people will make their voices heard.

Messaging: Consistency and Control

There was a rigorous effort to maintain the tone and consistency of email messages, especially those that were sent from Obama himself. The email team followed the campaign trail closely; anything Obama said was fodder for future emails. Short-term messaging, such as responses to specific comments made by Clinton or McCain, had to be balanced with the long-term messaging of hope, action, and change. *"Early on we learned that email could not only be a useful tool but a powerful vehicle to drive action,"* Geer recalled.

Before Barack Obama had a presence on social networks, email was the primary tool responsible for driving the message, especially when things didn't look so good. During the primaries, when the campaign experienced some devastating losses, the emails reported on the situation with frank honesty. They contained information about key demograph-  ics, calculated gains and losses, and shared the findings with subscribers. Eventually, including this type of data in emails became a strategy touchstone. This information was always sent to subscribers first, before the press, allowing the campaign to build an intimate relationship with supporters who are *"in the know."* It also allowed the campaign to control the information that was sent out to supporters. *"Messaging control gave us the power to make the average person just as powerful and informed as the media,"* Geer said. *"Often times [email was] faster than the media could distribute the news."*

On September 24, 2008, John McCain announced he would suspend his campaign in order to focus his attention on the legislative response needed to address the mounting economic crisis. He proposed delaying the first debate, set to take place on September 26, 2008, until the government had made some progress in dealing with the situation. Obama vehemently opposed the idea, insisting that *"this is exactly the time when the American people need to hear from the person who, in approximately 40 days, will be responsible for dealing with this mess."* Other proposed suggestions included having the vice presidential debates instead or having Obama hold a town hall in the event that McCain didn't appear. Throughout all the confusion, the campaign used email to keep their supporters updated on the status of the rapidly evolving story, ensuring that they were informed. McCain declared his intent to participate and debate went forward as planned.

From: Jon Carson
Subject: **Debate Timeline**
Date: September 25, 2008

Barack is moving ahead with plans for Friday's debate. The election is less than 40 days away, and the American people deserve to hear directly from the candidates about how they intend to lead our country. You're invited to join a Debate Watch Party in your community and discuss the issues that are most important to you and your family, friends, and neighbors."

From: Barack Obama
Subject: **Message from the debate**
Date: September 27, 2008

I just finished my first debate with John McCain. Millions of Americans finally got a chance to see us take on the fundamental choice in this election—the change we need or more of the same. I will provide tax cuts for the middle class, affordable healthcare, and a new energy economy that creates millions of jobs. John McCain wants to keep giving huge tax cuts to corporations, and he offered no solutions for the challenges Americans are facing in their daily lives. I will end the war in Iraq responsibly, focus on defeating al Qaeda and the Taliban, and restore America's standing in the world after eight years of disastrous policies. John McCain wants an unending commitment in Iraq and fails to recognize the resurgent threat in Afghanistan. Let's be clear: John McCain is offering nothing but more of the same failed Bush policies at home and abroad that he has supported more than 90% of the time in the Senate. Americans need change now, and I need your help to get the word out about this movement. In the coming days, it's going to be up to you to organize locally and reach the voters that are going to decide this election. Now's the time to make your voice heard.

From: David Plouffe
Subject: **In case you missed it**
Date: September 27, 2008

We put together an ad today that captures Barack's victory in last night's debate in 30 seconds. After his erratic and reckless response to the economic crisis, McCain needed a game-changer last night to restore his campaign. He didn't even come close. In a CBS News poll, uncommitted voters see Barack as the debate winner. When it comes to the economy, 66% say Barack would make the right decisions versus 42% for McCain. These are not the kind of reviews John McCain needed, but they show that Barack is offering the change we need. Barack broke through last night with voters who were watching—but we need to get the word out to the millions who didn't tune in. Will you watch our latest ad and make a donation to show your support?"

Motivation: Encouraging Reader Involvement

The email team helped raise over $500 million in online donations from 3 million individual donors. Email's main fundraising strategy was the use of what Geer described as "non-tests." The initiatives couldn't be called "contests" due to state lottery rules, but were basically small and repeated opportunities for small-amount donors to meet and interact with Barack Obama directly. For example if you donated a small amount you had the chance to receive front-row passes for the Obama rally in Grant Park on election night. This reinforced the message of empowerment and inclusion by replacing the power of Washington insiders, lobbyists, and special interest groups with the power of the American people. Traditionally, donors needed to raise hundreds of thousands of dollars to earn the privilege of mingling with a candidate, but now regular people were given the chance to sit down and talk with Obama in person. The enticing opportunity coupled with low financial barriers to entry incited many supporters to donate several times.

From: Barack Obama
Subject: **Front Row to History**
Date: October 31 2008

I want you to be there with me on election night when the results come in.

We're planning a big event that will include tens of thousands of supporters in Grant Park in downtown Chicago.

We're saving some of the best seats in the house for 5 people who make their first donation to the campaign before Sunday at midnight, as well as 5 people who have given before, but decide to make a donation one last time.

If you're selected, you can bring a guest, and we'll fly you in and put you up in a hotel for the night. You'll go backstage at the big event and—no matter what happens—you'll have a front-row seat to history as we celebrate the supporters who got us over the finish line.

Any donation counts—whatever you can afford. Show your support at this crucial time with a donation, and you could join me on election night:

https://donate.barackobama.com/frontrow

This movement for change has been a testament to the power of ordinary Americans coming together to achieve extraordinary things.

I look forward to having you there on election night.

Thank you,

Barack

Meaningful Content: Delivering Relevant Information

Over the course of the campaign, an astounding one billion emails were sent out to supporters across the country. The Obama team took the impersonal tactic of mass emailing and infused their messages with relevant and customized content for readers. Each type of email, whether a fundraising message or a call to action, was thoroughly tested for response and clickthrough rates. *"Everything you got—the sender name, subject line, content, layout, images—was tested,"* said Geer. Emails were even scheduled to be sent out at times when recipients were most likely to open them. Testing was done by the campaign's analytics department, who worked closely with the email team to optimize their voter outreach rates.

Geer insists that the frequency of emails sent was offset by the customized content that each supporter received. He wasn't concerned with voters feeling overwhelmed by the multitude of ways (phone, email, text) that they were being contacted by the campaign so long as it got them out to vote on November 4. There were some complaints from people receiving too many emails but for Geer it was a trade off. *"We knew that we could survive a certain amount of churn (fatigue combined with deliverability failures) because of our list growth.*" Campaigns are all about short-term wins no matter what the cost. This is an important distinction for corporations who want to form an ongoing relationship with consumers rather then a political campaign with a finite expiry date.

The campaign refined the microtargeting tactics used by the Republicans and hypersegmented their emails based on three factors: location, important issues, and donation history.

LOCATION

Emails used a recipient's zip code to determine location and included information about local grassroots events. This made the election more real for many supporters, since it brought the fight into their own backyards. State emails contained information about media campaigns occurring in the area, and provided supporters with the information needed to contact their local media outlet and political representatives about a particular issue. This proved to be very effective when dealing with Republican-leaning media outlets, as supporters could be instantly mobilized to collectively respond to smears or negative ads launched by the opposition. Strategically, this allowed the campaign to leverage their base by finding and using their most active supporters to take action on their behalf. Even if a state only contained 500 eager and motivated organizers within a population of thousands, 500 calls into a local radio or television station was more than enough to get the outlet's attention.

Segmenting emails by location helped local field offices locate highly active volunteers who could be recruited to help with official campaign efforts. It also paved the way for field staff to build strong networks in new states. When the campaign entered a state for the first time, the email list was used to identify users who had used my.barackobama.com to organize for Obama independently. Those names were given to field offices who were able to tap into existing networks of motivated volunteers rather than having to start from scratch. This gave the Obama team an

> **ON ELECTION DAY, SUPPORTERS** received an email that included the names of five likely Obama voters in their neighborhood who they could contact and remind to vote.

incredible head start since the email team was able to provide a list of volunteers with a recorded level of commitment. Geer says they were in uncharted territory. *"Nobody was doing what we were doing."*

IMPORTANT ISSUES

When signing up to receive email on the Obama site, subscribers could choose from a list of issues that really mattered to them. This ensured emails contained information that the reader would find interesting and share with family and friends. For example, an Obama supporter who had a family member enlisted in the army was more likely to be interested in Obama's Iraq exit plan. By providing them with that information, the supporter became more knowledge-able and was better able to share that information with their social network. This turned Obama supporters into "Issue Ambassadors," using their existing passion about a topic to share information with people who trusted their opinions. Voters were more likely to trust information coming from a friend or family member than a stranger on the phone or a television ad. Obama helped people spread his message of change by empowering them with the information they needed to speak confidently and accurately about his policy stances.

DONATION HISTORY

The last and most important factor in hypersegmenting was the sup-porter's donation history. Campaign emails took into account how much a voter had already donated to the campaign and how long ago the contribution had been made. This ensured that any requests for donations were made respectfully. It would have been inappropriate to send out an urgently worded request for a donation to someone who had recently contributed twice to the campaign. Segmentation also allowed the campaign to see which voters had already achieved the individual donation limit and remove them from further requests for financial donations.

SOCIAL MEDIA LESSONS

Team Email was able to support the campaign's mandate that online organizing equal offline action by providing voters with customized information about relevant issues coupled with local events taking place in their neighborhood. By November 2008, the campaign's email list contained 13 million addresses, compared to 3 million collected by John Kerry and 600,000 gathered by Howard Dean. The list was regularly screened to ensure that lobbyists or special interest groups had not subscribed.

MOBILIZATION — Each email that is sent out from an organization should have a purpose. Specifically, how consumers should respond to the communication. Do you want them to talk about your brand? Become aware of a new product? Share their feedback? Create some content? The desired outcome of the email should be clearly defined and the call to action must be stated in a way that's easy to understand.

MESSAGING — Pay close attention to the tone of all email communication. Short-term objectives, such as dealing with difficult economic times, must be balanced with longer-term communication objectives that reinforce brand values. The key is to vary the content but keep the tone and theme consistent. The campaign used a multitude of sources including Obama's speeches and interviews with the press as well as statements from the opposition to craft emails that remained true to the tone and style of the campaign. Email communication can also help an organization control the message by making it possible to contact consumers directly, bypassing the filter of mainstream media.

MOTIVATION — The idea of incentives has been a consistent theme throughout this book and email is no exception. Team Email used incentives to encourage readers to subscribe to emails.

MEANINGFUL CONTENT — Information overload has become a common side effect in today's online world; it has become increasingly difficult for companies to get any content in front of consumers. With e-newsletters, special offers, press releases, and spam, inboxes are expanding while attention spans are shrinking. To get their message across, companies must provide meaningful content that is relevant to consumers.

SPOTLIGHT

Tim Fullerton,
STATE/REGIONAL EMAIL MANAGER

JOINED THE CAMPAIGN: August 2008

ON HIS ROLE: "I managed the state-based email program. So any email request from a state office was coordinated."

ON BEING A PART OF THE NEW MEDIA TEAM: "It was the most intense and energizing work experience that I've ever had. In new media, specifically Team Email, it was seven days a week, sixteen-hour days, a go go go mentality. I've never experienced anything like that before. Every waking moment was devoted to a specific cause and it was amazing."

ON WORKING ON TEAM EMAIL: "It was a high-pressure environment, because you knew that thousands of people would be looking at what we were sending out. We were representing the presidential campaign. I felt very invested, because on our team we took a lot of pride in having a powerful message with no error. We worked together every hour of the day and we formed a strong bond. I still consider myself good friends with everyone on the team. Many of us still talk weekly, or even daily. When someone was tired, someone else would pick up the slack. We were all good friends by the end; it was like a family relationship. We would joke sometimes and other times it was serious and it was a tight bond."

ON BARACK'S WIN: "It validated everything we did, all the long hours, being away from friends and family and not having a day off, it was all worth it. It was the most rewarding experience of my life."

ON THE INAUGURATION: "Standing near the Capitol hearing the president being sworn in, it was a huge sense of accomplishment and pride. Seeing how happy everyone was, and sensing how ready America is for the next four years, it was incredible to think that I had played even a small part. Seeing Obama thank the staff for their hard work was a really happy moment; it felt really great to be recognized."

ON HIS FAVORITE CAMPAIGN MOMENT: "I was at my desk on Election Day, still monitoring to see if we had to send out more emails encouraging people to vote. I stood, because it was a lot easier to talk to the rest of the team, especially if we had to act fast. We needed to be prepared to move very quickly to draft and send an email depending on how the election was progressing. I looked up at one point and Spike Lee was standing right there. He said 'Hey man,' and shook my hand and asked if he could take a picture of us. It was really cool that someone like him would want a picture of us at work!"

ON THE "SLOW CLAP": "Anytime somebody was heading out to the field, which became a common occurrence the closer we got to Election Day, they were always saluted with a slow clap. Someone starts off clapping slowly, and soon everyone joins in and the clapping becomes faster until it's loud applause. It was a nice send-off for people, and it always made us laugh."

ON LESSONS LEARNED: "Email is a really good tool for reaching your supporters. Develop a strategy where you look at the data and see how readers are reacting to your messaging. Have strong analytics and consult them often."

TIM'S MESSAGE : "I truly believe that this administration is going to follow through on what they've said. I'm very hopeful after being in D.C. for the inauguration and seeing the change in attitude. D.C. isn't known as an enthusiastic place. I'm looking forward to the next four years to see the people being brought into the process."

9 *Text Messaging & Mobile*

C U @ THE RALLY

MOBILITY WAS ANOTHER NEW FRONTIER explored by the Obama team. The text messaging program was rolled out by Scott Goodstein, Obama's Director of External Online Organizing and Mobile, in June of 2007. Both Hillary Clinton and John Edwards also had an SMS component, but neither were as extensively integrated as Obama's efforts. The Obama mobile platform included supporter-made Obama wallpapers and ringtones that remixed Barack's quotes on healthcare and the war in Iraq. Text messaging was a new medium with several complicating factors including the fact that many users paid for incoming SMS messages. Texting provided an opportunity to connect with a certain segment of voters, particularly rural areas where people relied on the technology more heavily. This aspect of digital communications seems to have been completely overlooked by John McCain.

In a *Washington Post* interview, Goldstein described the importance of text messaging. *"To me, texting is the most personal form of communication,"* he said. *"Your phone is with you all the time. You're texting with your girlfriend. You're texting with your friends. Now you're texting with Barack."* The campaign used incentives to kick-off text messaging involvement. Users who signed up to the campaign's text messaging list received free campaign gear like buttons and bumper stickers. *"Millions of Americans relying on cell phones are cutting the cords to their landlines,"* Goodstein wrote on his MyBO blog in June. *"This new service is essential for us to communicate with a growing number of Americans where they're at."*

Supporters who signed up for SMS updates from the campaign received a variety of text messages including rally information when Obama was in their home town. The Obama campaign was the only one to segment its text messaging database by region, allowing them to target supporters in specific states. Text messaging strategy also included recruiting to help get out the vote, requests for donations, and announcing that Barack had chosen Joe Biden as his VP.

*"Finally a way for politicans to annoy you in restaurants
and movies theatres."*
- JON STEWART, DAILY SHOW, ON OBAMA'S RINGTONES.

In this chapter we'll discuss some of the learnings from the Obama
text messaging strategy:

ALWAYS LET USERS OPT IN — All aspects of the campaign's text messaging program depended on voluntarily offered information. This
established the Obama team's respect for supporters' personal digital
space and ensured that they delivered information to those who
genuinely wanted it.

CREATE A CONVERSATION — The Obama team was unique in its use
of SMS text messaging because the campaign staff responded to
inquiries and feedback.

PORTABLE ENGAGEMENT — The campaign's innovative iPhone application made supporting Obama easy everywhere you went.

Always Let Users Opt In: Choosing to Engage

The campaign used texting as a
platform to grow it's database. The
most important part of the texting strategy was the emphasis on
having users opt in to the SMS
list. Users had to sign up for the
program, and indicate that they were willing to receive updates from

the Obama mobile team. Once they had subscribed, supporters could also choose to provide additional personalinformation. Those who opted in with their zip code received geo-centric updates of events happening in their area.

Most text messages involved an ask, a specific call to action. Supporters were asked to watch the debates, to attend a rally, or to send feedback about a particular issue. A subscriber could decide to stop receiving updates at any time and Obama staff regularly scanned incoming text messages for any user who expressed unhappiness at being contacted.

Rallies were an excellent opportunity to increase the SMS database. At one rally during the primary in South Carolina, Jeremy Bird, the state field director, asked the 29,000 people who had come out to see Obama and Oprah Winfrey to each text "SC" to 62262 (which spells Obama) if they wanted to get involved in the campaign.

> *Obama was the only Democratic candidate who secured a personalized short code of 62262, which spelled his name. The other candidates relied on a randomly generated shortcode to engage supporters. Clinton used 70007, and Edwards, code was 30644.*

Thousands responded and the SMS list grew. Goodstein used these numbers to follow up encouraging involvement in phonebanking, canvassing and getting out the vote campaigns. The mobile strategy played a role in helping Obama win South Carolina by 28 points. Goodstein spent three weeks in South Carolina overseeing the program and studying how text messaging could be applied to all voters, not just the youth demographic.

In addition to building trust and showing respect to the community, an opt-in system was more effective as it delivered content to those who were interested in the information, increasing the likelihood of response and engagement.

Create a Conversation:
It's a Two-Way Street

The campaign made an effort to connect with voters by conversing with them instead of just broadcasting information. Texting formed a two-way relationship, staffers and volunteers responded to supporters who asked questions via SMS on particular issues or to find out where their voting location was. *"We will use text messaging to ask for your opinions and advice and give you the ability to request information from the campaign,"* Goodstein wrote. SMS comments were routinely mentioned on the blogs and various social networks.

> *Less than a week until Election Day on Nov. 4th! Barack needs your help. REPLY to this msg with your 5 digit ZIP CODE for local Obama news and voting info.*
> *– Text message from Barack Obama, Oct. 30, 2008, 2:53 EST*

A college student in Florida who donated $20 sent the following text with his contribution: *"When I got the text about the debate tonight, a few friends and I decided to stay in to watch instead of going out,"* he wrote. *"I'm sure you understand what it means for a college student, such as I, to part with their 'beer money' but here is the money I didn't spend because we watched your debate tonight. I hope it serves you well."*

During the CNN/Youtube debate in July 2007, the campaign received 600 SMS messages of ideas, stories and feedback. Texting was another way that the campaign could take advantage of people's social networks as it was easy to forward a text to friends and family. The campaign would often text supporters asking for volunteers to help with an upcoming rally or event. Enough time was built into outgoing text messages to ensure that supporters could forward the message to their family and friends quickly and efficiently.

> *2.9 million people received the campaign's Text message announcing Joe Biden as Barack's running mate.*

Goodstein also launched Obama Mobile, a website designed for mobile devices where users could easily access campaign information from the convenience of their smart phone.

"People who love their country can change it! Make sure everyone you know votes for Barack today. For voting info call 877-874-6226 or VoteForChange.com."
– Text message, Barack Obama , Nov. 4, 2008, 3:28 p.m. EST

Engagement on the Go: The iPhone Application

Barack Obama was the first political candidate to create an iPhone application that made it simple and easy for supporters to engage in

campaign activities anywhere they went. The free downloadable application was coded by Obama volunteers in just under three weeks and helped transform the iPhone into a powerful and portable field office. The application was introduced on October 2, 2008, with only 33 days remaining before the general election. 95,000 supporters installed the application and 11,191 of them made 41,075 calls.

The application had several features that would help supporters organize on behalf of the campaign:

- Call Friends
- Receive Updates
- Local Events [using GPS]
- Get Involved
- News
- Media

- Issues
- Countdown
- Donate Now

Here we discuss a few of these in more detail.

CALL FRIENDS

Phone calls were one of the most effective ways of connecting with potential voters and volunteers. Engaging people in conversation about campaign issues was a time intensive task that required a lot of man power. Traditionally, scores of volunteers would gather in a field office and tackle a list provided by staff.

The "Call Friends" feature helped facilitate phone calls, but with a twist: it relied on the caller's own personal network. The application accessed a caller's address book and organized contacts by key battle ground states. The application kept track of who had been called to prevent supporters from calling the same person twice. After each call a small screen popped up giving the user the option of reporting the results. Was the contact an Obama supporter? Were they interested in volunteering? Did they have any questions? The results were transmitted directly to field organizers who could then quickly follow up and get a real-time snapshot of the political landscape in a particular area.

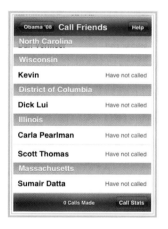

The application helped mitigate the impersonal nature of phone-banking by letting supporters reach out to their own network of family and friends. It also meant the people being called were likely to be more receptive to a call from a friend than from a stranger. As motivation, supporters could easily see how many calls they had made relative to other application users nationwide.

NEWS

The news function pulled an RSS feed of press releases and official statements from the campaign. A button allowed users to quickly shift between national and local press releases. Each news story contained a short summary, with a link to the full article online and an option to email to the contacts of a user's address book.

With the avalanche of information and the speed at which new issues emerged, this feature provided a quick and easy way to cut through the clutter and let people know Obama's stance on various issues. It also consolidated all of the campaign's statements in an easy to access location that supporters could refer to whenever they needed more information.

MEDIA

This feature allowed the campaign to capitalize on one of their greatest assets, Obama's charisma and eloquence – two things that could

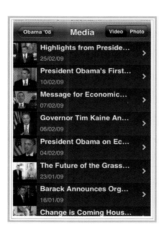

never be captured through an impersonal text-only press release. A button at the top of the screen allowed users to shift between videos and photographs. Each video had a brief text description of the subject matter, and was organized by searchable tags. There was a direct link to the Obama YouTube channel and the option to email any video to the contacts in the iPhone's address book. If a user decided to email someone a video or image, the application opened a new email message that contained the text:

"As a fellow supporter of Barack Obama and Joe Biden, I thought that the following story might be of interest to you." The application signed off with a link to the Obama application.

The media clips, speeches, and interviews gave supporters a chance to keep up to date with all the media released by the campaign and in the process get to know Obama. Additionally, it gave supporters a convenient way to share these clips by having them available all the time. I myself have pulled out my iPhone to show a favorite speech video, and I definitely appreciated the convenience of having them all in one place and searchable.

ISSUES

Issues was a feature that provided information about all of Obama's positions on issues ranging from his tax plan to environmental policies. The material was written in bite-sized chunks that were locally hosted. For example, here is what the application has to say on the issue of ethics:

The Problem

* Lobbyists Write National Policies

* Secrecy Dominates Government Action

* Wasteful Spending is Out of Control

Each headline was accompanied by a short one, or two–sentence explanation. This was followed by an overview of Barack's approach to addressing the issue, listed in bullet points. Then, a listing of Barack Obama's voting record on how he had addressed the particular issue in the past was provided, including concrete examples. Users could choose to download a full PDF that delved into the issues on a deeper level, as well as a link to any of Barack's speeches where he had talked about that particular subject. Users could also choose to fill out a form to submit their information and contribute their ideas and thoughts on any of the issues.

This empowered users to feel confident representing Barack because they knew that they had a wealth of information at their finger tips when they were discussing or defending his policies with others. Additionally, it ensured accuracy because it was a fast and easy way to get the facts—directly from the campaign.

SOCIAL MEDIA LESSONS

The real power of the mobile application was in its ability to integrate other social media aspects of the campaign. Text messages often included links to the Obama website. The Obama website also made it extremely easy to subscribe to text messaging online.

ALWAYS LET USERS OPT IN — Companies who are seeking to build realtionships through mobile applications must honor the trust that consumers have placed in them. Being transparent about any costs associated with a subscription, providing a clear explanation of what the consumer can expect to receive and how often, explicitly asking for their permission and making it extremely easy to unsubscribe are essential to a successful mobile campaign. Purchasing existing lists of consumer phone numbers will only aggravate them and create a negative brand experience.

CREATE A CONVERSATION — The emphasis should be on engaging, not lecturing your consumers. Ask questions, respond to feedback and always be helpful and polite.

ENGAGEMENT TO GO — The iPhone application provided a mobile portal where users could be connected to the latest campaign news no matter where they were. This took online engagement to a new level. With the rise of mobile applications and smartphones, new opportunities will emerge for organizations to provide value-added services for consumers in the real world. With increasingly sophisticated devices being released in the market, mobile technology will play an important role in upcoming political elections.

10 *The Blog*

THE CENTER OF THE OBAMAVERSE

"THE GLUE THAT HELD OUR RELATIONSHIPS WITH supporters together," is how New Media Director Joe Rospars describe the Obama blog network. It was the hub that captured all activities in the Obamaverse and shared them with the world. The blog was the campaign's content repository, a place where stories, videos, news, and pictures were captured and pushed out to Obama's many social network profiles.

The blog was used as a storytelling platform, and had a different tone and style than Clinton's and McCain's blogs. For one thing, it embodied the spirit of "Yes We Can" by showcasing the grassroots efforts of supporters from across the country. The blog profiled highly active

MyBO members, featured the latest campaign-made and user-generated videos, and provided a steady diet of Obama's campaign stops, speeches, and interviews. It was an easy way for readers to keep a finger on the pulse of the campaign. The blog helped to build a sense of online community by weaving campaign information with compelling supporter experiences and stories.

The blog was used to drive readers to the campaign's other online properties such as the YouTube channel, Twitter stream, or Flickr page, and to connect to the social networks. The Obama blog team wasn't worried about keeping readers exclusively on the blog; instead, the focus was on making sure that supporters could find a clear and concise campaign message no matter where they were.

In this chapter, we'll examine how the campaign's blogging strategy was used to integrate Obama's various online presences and maintain the MyBO's high visibility, with some specific observations about their use of the existing social network sites.

TELL A STORY — The campaign regularly profiled grassroots organizers and featured compelling guest blogs, creating a narrative that effectively communicated Obama's mandate without appearing preachy.

USE AN OLD FEATURE IN A NEW WAY — The blog team took the standard comment section on each blog post and transformed it into an area of lively discussion and debate.

PROVIDE A DIGITAL GATEWAY — The blog network encouraged supporters to subscribe to the campaign's email list and social network by publishing all campaign emails and providing blog tutorials of various MyBO features. This positioned the blog as a gateway for supporters to discover other ways to participate with the Obama movement.

LEAD BY EXAMPLE — Obama's desire for a more inclusive political process could be seen in the blogging team's effort to publish content and feedback provided by supporters. Their dedication and attentiveness to supporters reinforced through example the philosophies that guided the campaign.

Tell a Story

SUPPORTER SPOTLIGHT

In addition to the official Obama HQ national blog, there were state-specific blogs and constituent-specific blogs such as Students for Obama, Women for Obama, Environmentalists for Obama, and so on. The HQ blog often pulled posts from the state and constituent blogs into its own feed. Sam Graham-Felsen, Director of Blogging, was one of the earliest additions to the new media team and it was through his eyes that readers experienced the first stages of the campaign. The 27-year-old was a writer for *The Nation* and joined the campaign shortly after publishing an article about Obama's online popularity with young people. *"I wanted to be a part of the campaign instead of just writing about it,"* he said.

Graham-Felsen regularly profiled donors and campaign supporters from all walks of life. Profile posts included a picture of the supporter and a list of the reasons why they were supporting Barack. The blog was also used as a platform to promote and spread creative ideas by sharing noteworthy fundraising or canvassing events that inspired readers to get involved.

Being featured on the blog was an accomplishment that many supporters were very excited to show off. Proud grassroots organizers and donors shared the link on all of their social networks, bringing in new readers who now had a personal connection to the campaign through someone they knew. Often, seeing the face of a friend or neighbor on the official Obama blog motivated readers to get involved. In addition to national recognition on the official blog, featured projects usually received financial support once they were showcased on the site.

GUEST POSTS

The HQ blog also featured guest posts from prominent politicians who shared their perspective on the campaign. They included former U.S. Senator Harris Wofford, who served in the Kennedy Administration and helped to launch the Peace Corps. *"I haven't felt like this since the days of high hopes with John Kennedy, Robert Kennedy, and Martin Luther King, Jr.,"* he wrote. *"Barack Obama has picked up the torch that they lit."*

Wofford shared the story of John Kennedy who was campaigning in Ann Arbor, Michigan in 1960. He spoke to a group of 10,000 people, mainly university students, about the cost of ensuring a peaceful America. *"How many of you are willing to spend years in Asia, Africa, and Latin America?"* he asked the crowd. *"Our future depends on your willingness to do that."* After that speech a group of 250 students founded the group Americans Committed to World Responsibility and signed a petition documenting their willingness to participate in the peace effort overseas should Kennedy introduce such a program. It would be the inspiration for the Peace Corps, which was officially formed on March 1, 1961.

Wofford's example highlighted the importance of accountability, organizing, volunteerism, and patriotism without sounding condescending or preachy. It was a perfectly pitched call to action that resonated with readers. *"Kennedy's Peace Corps never reached the size and impact that we hoped for. We lost that opportunity, but the door to great new opportunities to serve at home and abroad is being opened again today,"* he continued in his post. *"Are you ready to be a part of history?"* The former senator finished off with a message that encapsulated the heart and soul of the campaign. *"The country needs you not only to answer his call to action,"* he wrote, *"but to be creative in your own right to discover the best way to serve and to build a better country and a better world."*

Use an Old Feature in a New Way: Leveraging the Comments Section

The comments section of each blog post became a vibrant platform for debate and discussion. Exchanges were usually hopeful, sometimes heated, and always interesting as a veritable culture emerged in the threads section. Each blog post would receive hundreds of replies as members of the community weighed in and shared their opinions. The campaign specifically fostered debate through open threads—posts devoted entirely to discussions in the comments section, usually on holidays or days of distinction. Sometimes there would be a theme to the open thread, for example, discussing what Martin Luther King, Jr. Day means to you, or supporters would simply be encouraged to share whatever they had on their minds.

This was a valuable way for the campaign staff to feel the pulse of the community and to get a clear sense of what readers were thinking about. The comments section (and the rest of MyBO) were self-moderated—each reader had the option to flag a post as offensive or inappropriate. Flagged content would then be reviewed by a member of the Obama team and action would be taken depending on the severity of the offense (a warning versus being removed from the site for violating the terms of service). This job was shared by the MyBO staff and volunteers who would spend hours every day wading through the content to make sure the site remained inclusive and welcoming. To be banned from the site you had to violate the term of service and act in a disrespectful way online. For example, using racial slurs or profanity, or deliberately being disrespectful to other MyBO users were all grounds for a warning; repeat offenders were kicked off the site. Any type of implied violence or threat of violence toward Obama was grounds for immediate expulsion from MyBO and the user's information was passed on to the authorities.

The blog allowed users to embed links and URLs in their comments, including links to their fundraising pages. This enabled supporters to leverage their online relationships into donations through the creation of small competitions. For example, undirected by the campaign, a friendly competition for who would be the first person to comment on a blog post emerged. The winner would include a link and the rest of the group would then donate a few dollars to that person's personal fundraising page.

An interesting practice emerged in the community in reaction to offensive comments that were posted anonymously on the blog. A supporter would take the offender to task via the comments section, usually including a link to correct any misinformation. The supporter would then add a link to their own fundraising page. Other users would post comments such as, *"I am going to show how much I disagree with your remarks by donating to this campaign."* Essentially, the Obama online community was carrying on the empowered feelings of hope and change by turning a negative experience into fuel for positive support.

Frequent readers of the blog built friendships and congregated daily to discuss their support of the campaign. The comments section became a digital water cooler, a regular meeting place to catch up and share information about the campaign or their daily lives. Tidbits about their personal canvassing experiences, favorite Obama moments, and reactions to debates and interviews fueled the excitement and passion felt on MyBO.

Provide a Digital Gateway: Republishing Emails and MyBO Tutorials

The campaign used the blogs as another platform to publish Obama's emails and focused on educating users about the various MyBO tools at their disposal if they chose to support the campaign.

EMAIL PLATFORM

Sam Graham-Felsen and the rest of the blog team also republished all official Obama emails that were sent out to supporters. This allowed the information to get passed on to people who read the blog but weren't on the Obama e-mail list. This practice also enticed readers to sign up for email updates and kept regular blog readers updated on campaign happenings. From a communications standpoint, posting the emails was about repetition and ensuring that readers were aware of all the content being created by the campaign.

MYBO TUTORIALS

The blog, which enjoyed a large regular readership, was also used to increase awareness and usability of the new tools that were being introduced on MyBO. Graham-Felsen introduced a blog series titled "Eight in '08," where he profiled eight different MyBO tools in depth and showed readers how to use them. For example, he walked readers through the process of uploading an event to the events section and offered tips on how to make their listing comprehensive and enticing to other voters. This produced a reservoir of knowledge available to users who might not have actively searched for that information in the tutorial section.

Lead by Example: Soliciting Content

The blog team also encouraged users to share their campaign experiences by inviting them to submit their own content. The blog had a weekly feature where the campaign would round up an assortment of user-submitted photographs of supporters organizing for the Obama. This was a great way to share the enthusiasm felt by supporters from across the country by rewarding them publicly for their hard work. The blog was also used to circulate content created by the other new media departments. Videos from Obama's official YouTube channel and pictures from the Obama Flickr site were reposted on the blog. This provided another platform for the content and exposed supporters to the other social networks where the campaign had a presence.

The blog team also took comments and feedback that were submitted on other social networks and blogged about them. The campaign would pick interesting conversations and repost them to the blog to drive readership and increase the online buzz. For example, on August 23, 2007, the campaign blog posted some of the reactions from several social networks regarding Barack's appearance on *The Daily Show*.

FROM THE OBAMA BLOG

Sarah in New York City texted us: "Just watched the recording and speaking as a student, the U.S. had lost that lovin' feeling but Barack has brought it back!"

Julie in Seattle wrote us through Barack's Facebook page and wrote, "WOW! You are the first politician... that has given me hope for our country. ... Thanks and keep up the fight."

Johanna from Oregon texted: "Obama just makes sense when he talks. He doesn't talk down to people and is refreshingly honest. TDS is the perfect venue for him!"

Julie from Chicago wrote us through Barack's MySpace page: "I turned off the Cubbies to catch you on *The Daily Show* last night! It is so refreshing to see an honest, intelligent politician. Thanks for keeping it real and talking about the things that matter!"

Shawn from Palm Harbor, Florida wrote us through our MySpace page: "It was a great move to make an appearance on TDS. Airtime well utilized, sir. Next up, Colbert."

-Scott Goodstein, Aug 23, 2007, From HQ Blog

SOCIAL MEDIA LESSONS

TELL A STORY — The blog focused on creating a constant narrative with small arcs of stories through various initiatives and campaigns. There was always something different happening on the blog, from supporter profiles and group fundraising challenges to announcements about new tools or features. This kept the content fresh so that readers would keep coming back on a regular basis. A successful blog provides a compelling narrative that captures a reader's attention and interest. It goes beyond press releases and product updates; it finds the stories of the people interacting with the brand and shares them with the online community.

USE AN OLD FEATURE IN A NEW WAY — The blog team took the comments section and turned it into a vibrant online town square where people could form relationships and engage with each other. Take a fresh look at the features you are building for your users. Can they be used differently?

PROVIDE A DIGITAL GATEWAY — The blog team made a dedicated effort to use the official blog as a gateway to encourage additional supporter engagement. Organizations can follow suit by republishing emails, e-newsletters, and other communications on the blog as a way to keep readers informed of the various methods they can connect with you. This can be applied across platforms; for example, a newsletter can contain links to that month's most popular blog post to drive traffic to the site.

LEAD BY EXAMPLE — The blog embodied the mantra of "Yes We Can" by making the community and its participants the focus of the stories told. The campaign used the blog not as a traditional one-way broadcasting model, but as a means to actively solicit from the user base. The types of things you post about, the tone in which your posts are written, and the way you respond to comments are indicators of your true intent. Actions often speak louder than words. For example, insisting that your organization values customer feedback but limiting their ability to comment on your posts sends conflicting messages.

SPOTLIGHT

Molly Claflin,
NATIONAL BLOG ASSISTANT EDITOR

JOINED THE CAMPAIGN: June 2008

ON HER ROLE: I wrote for the national blog, and worked on the rapid response team fighting the anti-Obama rumors and smear campaigns. The goal of the blog was to help organize our supporters and get them excited about becoming more involved with the campaign. On the rapid response front, my job involved creating content for FightTheSmears.com, writing emails to help forward the truth about Obama, and creating some content for the anti-McCain websites discussing McCain's voting record and ties to the Keating 5 scandal.

ON LEARNING FROM EACH OTHER: Most of us had never been involved in a national campaign before. Some had never been very politically involved before. We had to learn together. So the Team Email guys would ask me for help wording sentences. I would ask the ad team to help me choose the most compelling stories for the blog. Ads would ask Email which ad design layout was best. And so on. I liked the fact that though we all had a job to do, we helped each other on a daily basis.

ON ELECTION NIGHT: I walked into Grant Park just 5 minutes before the election results became official. Just as I grabbed an American flag from the stage, CNN called the election for Obama. I was jumping up and down, screaming, and beaming from ear to ear. It's rare in your lifetime that you can accomplish something that has such a clear and tangible reward. After over a year of work on the campaign, suddenly you can watch all your hard work pay off in one monumental, indescribable second. One second, and you have changed the world.

ON HER FAVORITE CAMPAIGN MOMENTS: Hearing Tom Brokaw call Ohio for Obama. Meeting Joe Biden. Watching the debates together. Rooftop barbecues. Feeling like other people my age finally cared about politics. Waving an American flag in the air in Grant Park and feeling like we might have just saved the world.

MOLLY'S MESSAGE: The Obama campaign felt a lot like an unlikely dream. I first got involved with the campaign, assuming that I would eventually go to work for Hillary Clinton.

But then people started coming together. Millions of Americans became re-engaged in the political process, and took to the sidewalks in their communities, and set out to make a difference. And we did.

That's what we need to remember from the Obama campaign—that however unlikely something may seem, all it takes is all of us working together, lending our voices to the cause, and standing up to make that goal a reality. That's hope.

11 *Social Networks*

OBAMA EVERYWHERE

THE CAMPAIGN USED SOCIAL NETWORK SITES
to increase their messaging reach and create relationships with supporters outside of MyBO. Barack Obama recognized the opportunity to connect with specific demographics and was the first candidate to build profiles on social networks that targeted minority communities, including MiGente, BlackPlanet, FaithBase, and AsianAve. The idea was to bring the campaign into the online communities where voters were already spending time. *"Some people only go to MySpace. It's where they're on all day. Some only go to LinkedIn. Our goal is to make sure that each supporter online, regardless of where they are, has a connection with Obama,"* said Scott Goodstein, Director of External Online Organizing. Goodstein's team monitored and maintained Obama's social network profiles. *"Then, as much as we can, we try to drive everyone to our site."*

A profile on a particular social network could emphasize content that resonated with that particular audience. For example, in his FaithBase profile, Obama focused on the value he derived from his own faith. On GLEE, an online community for Gays, Lesbians, and Everyone Else, Obama highlighted his efforts to promote and support equality. From a more practical perspective, the campaign invited Flickr users to share their images of the campaign, knowing that the pictures would be of higher quality because the community is geared to photography enthusiasts and professionals.

"When it came to MySpace, we decided to take a leap. We decided to make the attempt to combine the organic support and community-building of a grassroots effort with the official campaign outreach efforts."
—Joe Rospars, May 2, 2007

The campaign demonstrated a nuanced understanding of almost every social networking platform. From MySpace's push for unique profile pages, to LinkedIn's network of small business owners, the campaign engaged with these sites accordingly, providing high-value services and features to their supporters. In this chapter we will examine the strategies employed by the campaign at four major social networks: Facebook, MySpace, LinkedIn, and Twitter.

Facebook

The campaign's Facebook presence included official profiles for Barack, Michelle, and Joe as well as ten additional profiles targeting specific demographics, such as Veterans for Obama, Women for Obama, and African Americans for Obama.

In another technological first, in March 2007 the Obama new media team developed an innovative Facebook application that harnessed the power of interactive data. This linked a user's MyBO account with their Facebook account, seamlessly importing their Facebook contacts into MyBO and publishing their MyBO activities onto Facebook's newsfeed. The Obama Facebook application allowed the campaign to transform each community member's list of family and friends into an audience for campaign activities. When a MyBO user updated his or her fundraising status or joined a group, that information was published to all their Facebook friends, creating awareness about campaign issues and even luring a few curious folks to MyBO for more information.

The small widget was added to a user's Facebook profile page, and contained a stream of the campaign's most recent videos and the latest news items. Users were not directed to an external site but could access the content immediately from Facebook and they could rate and comment on videos. Because it received high user rankings, Obama's campaign content became available to a supporter's extended social network and offered more campaign content and links to the Obama site such as MyBO and the official blog. With the click of a button, supporters could select specific friends or family members they wanted to share Obama content with: digital word of mouth. Because online organizing equals offline action, the widget identified all contacts who lived in the early primary/caucus states, and urged supporters to encourage their friends to vote.

> **OBAMA ON SOCIAL NETWORKS**
>
> Overall, the Obama campaign had a presence on sixteen social networks including:
>
> AsianAve • BlackPlanet • Digg • DNC PartyBuilder • Eons • Eventful • Facebook • FaithBase • Flickr • GLEE • LinkedIn • MiGente • MyBatanga • MySpace • Twitter • YouTube

The campaign turned the application into a digital yard sign, allowing users a new way to show their support.

MySpace

The campaign leveraged MySpace users' ability to customize their profile pages by providing supporters with an array of widgets, banners, and buttons.

MySpace would also represent one of the first social network stumbles for the campaign, when the Obama team clashed with a user who had created an unofficial profile for Barack Obama before the campaign had created an official presence. Inspired by Obama's 2004 Democratic National Convention address, Joe Anthony had created and maintained the MySpace profile for two years, and had built its base of contacts to thirty thousand online friends. Every day after working a full-time job, Anthony would patiently answer hundreds of messages from supporters and ensure that the site contained the most up-to-date information.

 In early 2007, Chris Hughes, Obama's Director of Online Organizing, contacted Anthony and the two made an arrangement to work together. In exchange for giving the campaign full access to the MySpace account, Anthony could continue to manage the site and would receive support from the campaign in the form of advice and access to content. The profile's friends list grew to 100,000 and then skyrocketed to 140,000 after MySpace featured Obama's profile.

By May 2007, Anthony workload grew to an unmanageable level, and he emailed the campaign asking for compensation. After some attempts at negotiation they were unable to reach an agreement and he changed the password and denied them access completely.

The loss of control of such an important online property was unacceptable for the new media team. *"Every day, MySpace was driving tens of thousands of people to the page on the premise that this was more or less our 'official' presence—yet we had no access to the content on the page, and no ability to be responsive to the thousands of messages coming in from supporters seeking information or action from the campaign,"* Joe Rospars wrote on the official blog in May 2007.

The campaign contacted MySpace, which gave the profile and URL myspace.com/barackobama to the campaign and allowed Anthony to transfer his contacts to another profile. Rospars acknowledged the less-than-ideal solution. *"At the end of the day, this is all new for everyone,"* he concluded in a blog post. *"We're flying by the seat of our pants, and establishing new ways of doing things every day. We're going to try new things, and sometimes it's going to work, and sometimes it's not going to work. That's the cost and that's the risk of experimenting."*

Barack Obama did call Joe Anthony to thank him for his efforts, which Anthony described as *"an honor."* Ultimately, this experience proved to be a valuable lesson for the campaign about the importance of securing official properties on social networks early on in the process, and about some of the implications of having an empowered and digitally savvy grassroots movement that feels ownership over the campaign. The Obama team's transparency in clearing things up allowed them to emerge from this incident unscathed.

LinkedIn

By understanding the different types of users who frequent various social networks, the campaign was also able to mine valuable information. For example, on LinkedIn, the campaign asked business professionals, *"How can the next president better help small business and entrepreneurs thrive?"* The campaign

received over 1,500 answers, the most replies ever on LinkedIn. In addition, because members of the community were business owners, entrepreneurs, and professionals, the answers came from the very people that Obama's economic policies would affect. Not only did this effort start a meaningful dialogue with small business owners, it was the equivalent of a large-scale, complex online focus group conducted at minimal cost to the campaign.

Twitter

ON ELECTION DAY, Barack Obama had 115,000 followers on Twitter. As of March 2009, Obama is the most followed person on the microblogging site, with over 424,584 followers. Twitter allows users to share short snippets of their lives in 140-character messages, and was used by the campaign to update supporters on Obama's whereabouts and election developments. Twitter updates, called tweets, contained links to live-streaming videos or new campaign ads. I found Twitter to be the most underutilized social

network used by the campaign. Twitter is powered by conversations between users, and the campaign only broadcasted information instead of engaging users in dialogue.

SOCIAL MEDIA LESSONS

BE WHERE YOUR CONSUMERS ARE — Social networks provide an excellent opportunity to engage with consumers in online spaces they frequent regularly. This allows customers to engage with brands and organizations online without having to visit the official site. A presence on social network site also makes it easier for customers to interact with an organization because they aren't forced to jump through the digital hoops of setting up a new account. If you successfully engage with a consumer on their preferred social network, you will have the added benefit of exposure to that person's extended contacts on the network.

MAKE SURE IT FITS — As a presidential candidate, Barack Obama had to reach out to all consumer demographics. For most companies I recommend a strategic fit: it might make sense for your company to be on Twitter but not on MySpace, or LinkedIn but not Facebook. Choose a social network based on your organization's goals and strategies for engaging in the space. It is better to be on one right network then on five wrong ones.

MEASURE ENGAGEMENT, NOT MEMBERSHIP — It is easy to get caught up in the race for more followers or online friends. However, the number of Facebook friends that your organization has means nothing if those people aren't engaged with your community. The value being generated from your social network presence is the barometer for success, not the volume. When entering a new online space, define how your organization will measure engagement: by the quality of the comments on the wall? The number of returning visitors? The length of time they spend on a page? Such metrics will give you better insight into your performance within that space than the number of members.

UNDERSTAND ONLINE SOCIAL ETIQUETTE — Each online community attracts a different type of person and enjoys a unique social code that governs the way members interact with each other. For example, Facebook and LinkedIn are sites where people usually add contacts they already know or have met in real life. On MySpace and Twitter, it is acceptable to approach or be approached by someone you have never met. Violating these conventions can offend users and give your organization a poor reputation. The easiest way to tune into a site's social guidelines is to create an account and be an observer for a few weeks. Listen and watch how other people engage with each other and ask questions if you're unsure. Above all else, when uncertain, always fall back on politeness and respect a person's online space.

TRANSFORM SOCIAL NETWORKS INTO DISTRIBUTION PLATFORMS — Organizations often create social network profiles and then find it difficult to update them regularly. You don't need to create new content for every single network you are on. For example, if you have a corporate blog, pull the RSS feed into your Facebook or MySpace profile page. Embed your YouTube videos on your blog and on every social network profile page. Send messages through microblogging sites such as Twitter to let people know about a new blog post or new video. Each social network can become a portal through which a customer can access a wide variety of information without having to leave the site. This ensures that your content is seen by more people, and can improve your search rankings.

EMBRACE INTERNAL AND EXTERNAL CONTENT — One of the most common pitfalls in corporate social media ventures is posting only internally created content, such as press releases, videos, and so on. Smart organizations post internal and external content. External content can be an industry-related report, a press clip about something interesting, a blog post from an online community leader, or a user-generated video. Posting this information not only makes your online presence more interesting but also integrates your site into the online community.

12 *Video*

UP CLOSE & PERSONAL

VIDEO WAS ONE OF THE OBAMA CAMPAIGN'S MOST effective tools because it capitalized on one of their greatest assets: the eloquence and charisma of Barack Obama. The video team was led by Kate Albright-Hanna, an Emmy-award winning producer who had previously worked in CNN's political division. Albright-Hanna met New Media Director Joe Rospars on the Howard Dean campaign—Rospars was a blogger, and she was filming a documentary. Recognizing the power of video from the beginning, Rospars had employed a videographer and screenwriter/producer team to create campaign footage from the early days of the race. Albright-Hanna wanted to shoot a documentary about Obama, and her interest was piqued when she discovered the campaign shot and produced its own video content. After submitting a proposal describing how Obama could effectively leverage video, she was offered a full-time position as Director of Video.

For Albright-Hanna and the video team, it was important to create content that resonated with people. It was a change of pace from the hyperformatted and ratings-focused newsroom Albright-Hanna was accustomed to. *"Here we don't worry about how many views our videos get. That's not a priority,"* she said. *"One of our goals is to get people talking about what's going on in their lives and why they're supporting Barack."* The videos brought the blog and email campaigns to life by providing a constant stream of meaningful stories that could be seen and shared with friends. From interviews with Iowa precinct captains to footage from rallies, the emphasis was always on amplifying the feeling of community by showcasing videos featuring the campaign's most passionate grassroots organizers. Albright-Hanna stressed the importance of user-generated videos, *"Early on, we wanted to capture the sense that this campaign is not just about Obama."*

YouTube gave the campaign the reach and distribution of a major television network—for free. It provided users with an almost unlimited volume of content available on demand, 24/7. Over the course of the campaign, the video team uploaded over 1,500 videos and the channel had over 20 million views. Obama supporters watched nearly one billion minutes of campaign footage. YouTube was the perfect holding tank for the campaign's footage. BarackTV also had a donate button where users could contribute anywhere from $15 to $1,000 using Google Checkout.

Types of Video

The Obama team used three different types of video: live-streaming, campaign-created, and user-generated.

LIVE-STREAMING VIDEO

Through live-streaming video, the campaign documented in their entirety many moments that would have been edited, shortened, or not covered at all by the media. Every stump speech and campaign stop, no matter how small, was filmed. Notices went out using Twitter and text messaging to let people know when a live-streaming event was going to take place. This gave supporters more opportunities to connect with the campaign, and see footage that revealed a side of Obama's personality that transcended media coverage.

CAMPAIGN-CREATED VIDEO

Albright-Hanna's team created a variety of videos that captured the spirit of the campaign. For example, the *"Signs of Change"* video included user-submitted pictures of supporters from every state holding up Obama "Change" signs. They also included interviews with supporters, event footage, and other creative and inspiring content to motivate people to register to vote. In total, the campaign's YouTube channel had more than 1,831 videos and 162,503 subscribers. The use of YouTube also made sense strategically because members could easily embed those videos in their Facebook page, blog, or other personal site.

USER-GENERATED VIDEO

The Obama team realized that the enthusiasm and passion of grassroots organizers and supporters could be more powerful then any slick marketing campaign. Supporters were invited to create and upload their own videos, which were then shared through the blogs and on BarackTV. This allowed the campaign to increase their bandwidth by sharing the responsibilities of video creation. It also ensured that the campaign had a constant supply of new content from places where the video team couldn't always be. Finally, it capitalized on the social aspect of video sharing: contributors passed the video to their friends and family, giving it a viral quality that might not have been present in an official campaign-made video.

The Value of Video

Video provided a tremendous value to the campaign in several ways.

ACCESSIBILITY FOR ALL

The video team made a consistent effort to listen to and incorporate user feedback. In June 2007, Tom Faar, a Gulf War Veteran asked the video team if they would make closed captioning available on campaign videos. *"When you're at war,"* said Tom, *"there are so many guns going off in your ears. So many of our veterans are deaf or hard of hearing and they really depend on closed captioning."* The Obama campaign became the first political campaign to offer closed caption-ing and Spanish captioning for their online videos.

REMIXING CONTENT

Uploading Obama's speeches to the web gave them longevity. It allowed voters who might not have discovered Obama until later in the campaign to review content that might have otherwise been inac-cessible. His "A MORE PERFECT UNION" speech in March 2008 and "YES WE CAN" concession speech from the New Hampshire primary, for example, had millions of views. Users could also take the content from the speeches and remix it into something new. By adding their own photos or music soundtrack, users turned many of the videos into something original. (Will.i.am set the "YES WE CAN" speech to music and created a viral hit that was viewed over twenty-six million times.) It also allowed supporters to produce their own campaign ads, which increased Obama's online exposure and presence.

DISTILLING BARACK'S MESSAGE INTO BITE-SIZED CHUNKS

While most of Obama's speeches were available in their entirety, many campaign videos were less than five minutes long—an ideal length for supporters to forward to their friends. Five minutes was short enough that it wouldn't demand too much of the viewer's time, but long enough to capture the essence of the hope/change/action mantra that defined so much of the campaign's rhetoric. The use of music, images, and video also captured the message of the campaign in an emotional way that might not have been possible with words alone.

LEVERAGING THE COMMUNITY'S RESPONSE

An important part of the YouTube community's philosophy is the ability to post a video response. Video responses on Obama's videos led to increased traffic, because when someone posted a comment on their own channel it would encourage those who came across that video response to link to the original speech to see what it was about. This capitalized on existing community behavior to increase traffic and visibility.

EXTENDING THE NEWS CYCLE

YouTube also had a huge impact on the coverage of both campaigns by hosting news clips that might have normally disappeared after one news cycle. This worked both for and against the Obama and McCain teams, as controversy didn't just disappear after a few days. Governor Palin's fumbled interviews with *CBS Evening News* anchor Katie Couric were edited and remixed by supporters into video clips and passed around virally online. Many popular talk-show segments were also uploaded, giving them a lifespan beyond the one-time broadcast. Supporters would then forward their favorite Jon Stewart or David Letterman joke to their friends and subscribers.

SOCIAL MEDIA LESSONS

BUILD A HISTORY — Use video to help new consumers get to know your brand or organization better. A video channel can show a more human or fun side to your organization. Upload all your television ads, media interviews, and anything that consumers would find interesting. Use consistent tags and titles to make your videos easy to find.

SPEAK DIRECTLY TO CONSUMERS — Online video can allow you to bypass traditional media and speak directly to consumers. It presents an opportunity to be honest and transparent with your viewers. Be genuine and authentic.

KEEP VIDEOS SHORT AND SWEET — Shorter videos have a better chance of being viewed in their entirety and, more importantly, of being forwarded to family and friends. Many organizations try to cram too much information into an online video, which irritates consumers. Instead, try breaking up large chunks of content into a series of smaller clips. Series are a great way of tackling complex issues and allowing viewers to engage with content in a digestible format.

SHARE YOUR CONTENT — Let users share and embed your content. Embedded content in someone's blog means more views. Also, if you don't embed your videos someone will find a way to steal them. Your organization then misses out on the ability for viewers to click back to your main page for additional information.

Zealan Hoover,
NEW MEDIA OPERATIONS INTERN

JOINED THE CAMPAIGN: August 2008

ON HIS AVERAGE DAY: I processed all the television and video ads that the paid media team produced, hosting them online, creating a webpage for them on MyBO, and then getting the URL to that page back to paid media so it could be distributed to the press and they could see the videos or listen to the ads on the website. Once they went public I also got them up on our YouTube account.

ON LANDING AN INTERNSHIP: I was determined to work for the campaign in the national headquarters in Chicago but it turned out to be harder to get in than I had expected. Over the spring primary season I had volunteered as much as my schedule allowed, making phone calls from home, door knocking on weekends, and sign waving after school, but as it was my senior year of high school I could not take any serious amount of time off. Ultimately it was Gray Brooks—a distant family acquaintance and Obama New Media staffer—who said that he could use me in Chicago and asked me how soon I could be there.

ON THE NEW MEDIA TEAM: The new media team was like one big family. There were constant pranks, people sleeping on our pink unicorn mascot, Click-Thru. Gray and I shared one tiny desk so we got to know each other quite well. Team Design adopted me since, at 18, I was the youngest one there, and I was away from home for the first time. It was really amazing having a surrogate family of sorts. By November, I felt like I had been living with them for years.

ON ELECTION NIGHT: I was kinda bummed because everybody else had HQ Credentials to get up front whereas I only had a General Admin Pass that would have me scrapping for a line of sight from behind tens of thousands. Luckily, a certain amazing fantastic friend of mine to whom I am forever indebted [Author's note: This was me!!] pressed a HQ credential into my hands just as I was about to leave the office!

ZEALAN'S MESSAGE: Anything is possible if we put our minds to it; it's just putting all of our minds to the same purpose that proves to be a challenge. If we can do that—rally around a common cause and ignore the petty differences—then we can really put our country back on track.

13 *Analytics and Online Ads*

DRIVING AND MEASURING TRAFFIC

WHILE THE CAMPAIGN WAS EXPERIMENTING
with new and innovative applications of social networking tools, the
new media team was focused on delivering results. The online advertising and analytics departments worked tirelessly to achieve this
goal. Online Ads placed banners, text ads, and display ads all over the
web to drive traffic to Obama's website. The analytics team studied
everything from page views to email open rates to provide an overall
snapshot of new media performance. In this chapter, we'll look at
the strategies behind driving and measuring traffic on a dynamic site
like barackobama.com:

THINK LIKE THE END USER — The online ads team anticipated popular
search terms and news-cycle targeted words to drive supporters to
the Obama website.

THE POWER OF ITERATION — The analytics team measured new media's
initiatives and recommended ways to increase effectiveness.

Think Like the End User: The Power of Search and Targeting

The online ad team would spent $16 million on
online advertising in 2008 alone, eclipsing Senator
McCain's' expenditure of $3.6 million. To get sup-
porters to visit the site, the online team had to
think like the end user and anticipate the search
terms and behavior that would lead to more site
traffic. Search-based ads were the foundation of
the campaign's online ad strategy because they
were so effective in recruiting new donors, volunteers, and supporters. A search-based ad is one or
two lines of text that appear when a user searches
for a particular word or phrase in an engine like
Yahoo or Google. The ads usually appear on the
search result page as "sponsored links" separate
from the regular search results.

To help meet its primary goal of recruiting new Obama supporters, the team bought search-based ads tied to a mix of news-cycle targeted words (Palin, McCain, economy) and frequently searched terms (Barack, Obama, vote, Democrat). New Media Director Joe Rospars described the return on investment as nearly 15 to 1. Display ads, graphics, or banners placed on a variety of websites and blogs were used less often. These promoted specific calls to action, such as subscribing to a text-messaging campaign.

Social networks also saw their share of online ads: the Obama team purchased $643,000 worth of Facebook ads over the course of the campaign. Online ads were purchased in smaller quantity on MySpace and BlackPlanet. The campaign also invested in advertising on blogs, with $149,000 spent with blogads, the popular advertising blog network representing 1,500 of the web's most popular blogs.

TOP 5 RECIPIENTS OF OBAMA CAMPAIGN ONLINE MEDIA SPENDING IN 2008	
Google	$7,500,000
Yahoo	$1,500,000
Centro	$1,300,000
Advertising.com	$947,000
Facebook	$643,000

Obama was the first political candidate to advertise in video games using Microsoft's gaming ad network, Massive. $94,000 was used to encourage early voting in popular games such as Burnout Paradise. These initiatives uncovered a wealth of untapped real estate that can be used by political candidates to engage a younger audience that might miss messages being sent through traditional mechanisms.

SPOTLIGHT

Jeff Lane,

INTERACTIVE MARKETING MANAGER, ONLINE ADVERTISING

JOINED THE CAMPAIGN: August 2008

ON HIS ROLE: I was the Interactive Marketing Manager responsible for search engine marketing and landing page optimization, part of the online advertising team in the new media department.

ON GETTING ON THE NEW MEDIA TEAM: I saw an article on a digital marketing website that mentioned the Obama campaign's was looking for interactive marketing managers. I applied for the position, even though the job posting was a month old. A month later, Andrew Bleeker, Director of Online Ads, called me and offered me the job. I quit my current job and relocated to Chicago.

ON THE NEW MEDIA TEAM: The team is a group of young, very smart, and highly driven overachievers. There was a shared sense of optimism and a passion to win.

ON THE IMPORTANCE OF COMPUTER SECURITY: We spent a lot of time around each other, simply as a result of the campaign hours. Every day, our team took a group photo. I haven't looked at them, but it was fun. Leaving your computer unlocked was a bad idea. The first time I did that, Gray Brooks changed my font and resolution settings so I couldn't read anything on my screen. There was a constant stream of funny and embarrassing emails "from" people who had forgotten to lock their computer.

ON ELECTION DAY: During the day, I had mixed feelings of nervousness, excitement, and optimism, but mostly I was hungry to win (and felt fairly confident that we would). I was working until about 10:00 p.m., so I was primarily concerned with performing my job. I didn't have time to reflect on the situation until we started walking to Grant Park.

Election night was the most memorable night of my life. Standing in Chicago's Grant Park, surrounded by coworkers who had become friends, and my family who had flown in for the occasion, I was overwhelmed by the moment—and I knew that my experience was being shared by millions of people around the world. It felt great—like we were on top of the world.

ON OBAMA'S ADVICE: Election night was my favorite moment, for sure. Visits from Michelle Obama and Joe Biden, and the phone calls from Barack, especially when he warned us against getting arrogant and overconfident. Good advice.

JEFF'S MESSAGE: This election wasn't just a win for Barack Obama, it was a win for the American people. It's time for us to move forward and confront our problems with courage, conviction, and determination. We've done it before, we can do it again.

Analytics: The Power of Iteration

Team Analytics was the Obama campaign's watchdog, monitoring and measuring everything from the effectiveness of online ads, to the open rates of emails. Using services like Google Analytics and Google Website Optimizer, the campaign gathered enough data to establish a solid understanding of where supporters were spending their time on the Obama site, and where and when to place the ads that would draw them there. Every email, text message, website visit, and online ad was also analyzed. Multiple variations of the same email were created to test the impact of a header, the value of embedding video versus audio, and having a donate button instead of a text link. This information was used to continuously refine the campaign's online communication strategy. Improvements and adjustments were made daily and the results could be seen in the improved conversion rates.

The analytics team was led by Dan Siroker, who had previously headed up the development of Google's browser, Chrome. Siroker's job was to find quantifiable ways to maximize voter outreach and donations. This was another new development in political campaigns, as this task had traditionally been outsourced to a vendor. The Obama camp had identified enough value in the service to have a team in-house.

Having attended Obama's speech at Google in 2007, Siroker was immediately struck by his authenticity and vision for a better America. *"I called my girlfriend and brother and left them enthusiastic voicemails about how this guy was the real deal and how I had never been in love with another man as much as I was that day,"* he posted on his blog. *"In the back of my mind I was a bit worried that this euphoria must have been similar to the euphoria felt by the masses who were persuaded to follow the ideologies of dictators and tyrants. I told myself to take time to make sure I was making the right decision, whatever that decision might be."* Dan picked up a copy of *The Audacity of Hope* and became convinced that participating in the campaign was the right thing to do. *"After hearing Obama speak about his ideas for how technology and innovation are going to help solve some of our country's biggest problems, I knew I could do more than just donate money. I would rather do my best trying to make a difference than do nothing and question myself after it's too late."*

The campaign embraced a philosophy of constant iterations by using the data they collected to instantly adjust and course correct on social media initiatives. This says a lot about the campaign's experimentation mentality, and how organizations can adopt a similar mindset. The campaign was always learning, using every method of online outreach as an opportunity to improve their processes. While many companies are not dealing with the condensed and finite timeline of an election, there is much to be learned from constantly testing and updating processes. Building agility and flexibility into internal systems can ensure that companies evolve with the technology and adapt to changes with their consumers instead of needing a massive technological overhaul every few years. This runs contrary to many corporate philosophies that state things must be perfected and refined before being released.

"It was similar to what I felt when I witnessed Steve Jobs announce the iPhone at MacWorld."
—Dan Siroker, Analytics Lead, after hearing Obama speak at Google in 2007

SOCIAL MEDIA LESSONS

THINK LIKE THE END USER — It's important to place yourself in your users' shoes. Their approach to navigating your site or searching for your products and services might not be what you expect. Asking family, friends, and colleagues to search for your site and observing the search words and terms they use can provide valuable insight into consumer behavior that you might have overlooked.

THE POWER OF ITERATION — Today, perfection is a luxury that competes with the speed of changing technology. Successful companies embrace their status as an ongoing work in progress, and strive to improve their processes. Corporations shouldn't jump on every bandwagon that comes along or change established processes on a whim, but they should constantly research the effectiveness of their email campaigns, e-newsletters, blogs, and so on, and find ways to make them better.

SPOTLIGHT

Jim Pugh,
TEAM ANALYTICS

JOINED THE CAMPAIGN: Summer 2008

ON HIS ROLE: I worked on the analytics team of the new media department. Our job was to work with the online data collected by the campaign and to (a) analyze and retrieve information needed by other members of the campaign, and (b) use that information to optimize the campaign's online presence. This typically involved a lot of programming using the campaign databases, as well as the application of statistical tools to improve the impact of our optimizations.

ON JOINING TEAM ANALYTICS: I decided fairly early in the election (December 2007) that I was interested in working with the Obama campaign. However, I was completing my PhD in robotics in Switzerland at the time, and it wasn't until summer 2008 that I was able to complete my experimental work and fly out to Chicago to get involved. Once I arrived, I met with several people working in new media at national headquarters and convinced them that I would be valuable addition to the department. I started working for the campaign full-time at that point, while simultaneously writing my PhD dissertation in the evenings and on weekends

ON WORKING WITH THE NEW MEDIA TEAM: Chaotic and collegiate are two words that come to mind; there were always a million things happening at once, and work often continued late into the night. Many of the staffers and volunteers had only just graduated from college, and I think this resulted in a work atmosphere not unlike those found at universities. People in the department were very open to discussing new, sometimes radical, ideas.

ON HIS REGULAR DAY: I would typically get to campaign headquarters between 9:00 a.m. and 10:30 a.m.; some of the others on my team would arrive as late as noon. However, it was very common to stay until midnight or later. There was remarkably little conflict, considering the high-stress nature of the situation; I think all of us were so focused on getting Senator Obama elected that it didn't seem worthwhile to get upset about the little stuff.

ON MAKING A DIFFERENCE: The night before the election, Alexander McCormmach (another analytics team member) and I stayed up all night preparing the caller/callee match data for the email that was sent out on Election Day. That one night may have had a greater impact on the election that just about all of my previous efforts combined; the email went out with contact information for one million sporadic voters. Even if only one percent of them were convinced to vote, that's ten thousand more people than we would have had otherwise, and without our overnight work, it couldn't have been sent. It feels good to know that you helped make a difference.

ON LESSONS LEARNED FROM THE CAMPAIGN: In my mind, there were two critical attributes that allowed the new media department to succeed. First was its management as a meritocracy; if you did a good job, you were given more responsibilities and authority, and new, capable people could get highly involved in a very short period of time. I think that this approach resulted in efficient, quality work. Second, people were willing and able to think outside the box; many of the successful online strategies employed during the election were unlike anything that had been done before in political campaigns, and this was due to the creative, progressive attitude of people in the department.

JIM'S MESSAGE: I feel like President Obama's election is a symbol of a new mindset that's emerging in the United States (and perhaps across the entire world). I think people are starting to see things from a more global point of view and at the same time realize that it's more important to get the big things done than to argue over the little things. I hope that what we helped to accomplish during the campaign is only the start of a continued growth that will persist in the years to come.

THREE

THE PRESIDENT

A NEW BEGINNING

PERSONAL EXPERIENCE

Election Day
Change has come to America

THE COVETED STAFF GRANT PARK TICKETS

ELECTION DAY WAS HERE!

I had made an unspoken agreement with Chicago that I would help get Barack elected, if it didn't snow in the city. In my opinion it was a fair and reasonable bargain and by election day the Windy City seemed to be cooperating. November 4th was an unusually warm day by Chicago standards. I thought it was a good omen that I could leave my jacket at home for the first time in weeks. I couldn't eat anything all morning. New Media, usually loud and rambunctious, was eerily quiet that day. Everyone was hunched over their computers monitoring the news. I felt my own anxiety shoot through the roof as I read about the thousands of voting problems that had already been reported. I did get a laugh when I saw Clickthru, he had come prepared for battle. The Design team had created a special election day outfit for him.

CLICKTHRU READY TO CHALLENGE THE REPUBLICANS

We received text messages and email from supporters across the country letting us know that certain polling locations were predicting an average waiting time of six hours! Our grassroots organizers really came to the rescue. They provided umbrellas where it was raining and also allowed voters to rest by standing in line for them. In headquarters, we shifted our efforts to getting out the vote, everyone was calling voters reminding them to get out and cast a ballot for Barack. Several people came up to me and asked me the same question in hushed tones. *"If we lose... how much room do you have at your place in Canada?"*

Crowds of people were already making their way towards Grant Park but we didn't know whether it would be a celebration, or a concession. I couldn't bear leaving the office until it was settled. I paced. I speculated. I found myself eating a gigantic cupcake that I neither craved not wanted for lack of anything better to do. I had just taken a big bite when I looked up to see the Director of Video, Kate Albright-Hanna, aiming her video camera right at me. I was mortified. *"Kate!"* I yelled. *"Promise me you won't put that in your documentary!"*

"Stress Eating, Exhibit one," she laughed. I immediately threw the rest out.

I heard an excited shout from behind me. *"The first polls are closing!"* Everyone gathered around and started counting down the last few seconds before the East coast polls closed. The results came in slowly. I was taking pictures on my iPhone and twittering my thoughts as the evening unfolded. It seemed as though the whole world was talking about this election online. I saw a tweet that made me exclaim in surprise. *"Fox News just called Ohio!"* There was a pause as everyone looked up at me with anxious expressions. *"For us!"* I added quickly. *"Fox News called Ohio, FOR US!"*

"What?!" Brian Sisolek from analytics looked at me disbelievingly. His fingers were already flying on his keyboard. *"It's not up on their site,"* he said, disappointed.

I was already scanning Twitter, *"They took it back!"* Fox News had declared Obama the winner in Ohio with only 3% of precincts reporting and then retracted their projection minutes later. Everyone groaned in frustration.

New Media Team Members react to good news

Luckily, their projection was soon confirmed by additional media outlets: Obama had won Ohio, the state that Karl Rove had proclaimed essential for McCain's campaign. The entire office erupted in a cheers, screams, applause, laughter and tears. People were hugging each other and jumping up and down. I remember Chris Hughes, who had been quietly watching the race, looking over at me and with a big smile and saying, *"Ok, now I can relax!"*

FINALLY FEELING LIKE WE JUST MIGHT MAKE IT!

After Ohio, the wins started pouring in. We finally felt confident enough to head over to Grant Park. We raced down to the trolley-bus that was shuttling campaign staff and guests to the Park. Once we were on board, we were escorted by Secret Service in sedans and Police motorcycles, all flashing their lights as we made our way through the city. As we approached Grant Park we were all stunned at the sheer number of people. A sea of people and American flags seemed to stretch out for miles and we weren't even inside the actual park yet. We entered from a back entrance, mere moments before the West coast polls closed. The mood was electric, filled with pent up excitement and joy. Everyone was just waiting for CNN to confirm the news on one of the gigantic screens.

ELECTION NIGHT AT GRANT PARK

New Media team members were running around, trying to find each other in the crowd. As the countdown to the results began, a group of us huddled together, counting along with the million people that showed up to Grant Park that night. I received texts and tweets from friends all over the world who were tuning in from their homes. I felt like the whole world was watching.

5...4...3...2...1 The West coast polls were closed. I will never forget how that moment seemed to stretch out forever. Then, silence, until on the screen a picture of Barack appeared with the words *"The President of the United States."* I felt the entire park explode with noise. I hugged Jesse, Carly, Molly and Jeff who were all around me. I was jumping and laughing and high-fiving people who were complete strangers. People were dancing. I heard someone call my name, and I turned to see Zelan, a Design Team Intern running towards me. At well over six feet he picked me up and spun me around in circles yelling, *"We did it! We did it!"* I can still recall the feeling of laughing and flying through the air.

Watching Barack during his acceptance speech, I almost burst with pride. I was happy for him, for the team, for the world. I couldn't believe that all of our hard work had actually paid off. I think most of us were still in shock. *"Did we do that?"* I kept hearing people asking each other. *"Is he really the President?"* Even after a landslide victory, Obama still made the effort to reach out to those who hadn't voted for him imploring them to participate in improving America. *"Is this what it feels like to have a President that can string together a sentence?"* I heard someone beside me ask in wonder. *"Because I can get used to this."* I just laughed.

OBAMA'S VICTORY SPEECH. CELEBRATING WITH MOLLY

The staff victory party was appropriately held in the Presidential Suite of one of Chicago's downtown hotels. As I poured myself a glass of wine and chatted with Team Email, I was suddenly exhausted. As more people arrived at the party, their cheer and energy was infectious and we all found our second wind. New Media Director Joe Rospars entered the suite and everyone applauded and cheered. *"Speech, speech, speech!"* We chanted until he finally agreed to say a few words.

He thanked everyone for all of their hard work and effort. *"Whatever happens with future elections, it's never going to be like this again,"* he said. *"This was the first campaign to do something so revolutionary, and when we look back on this campaign you can all say that you were a part of it."* After several hours of dancing, eating, drinking and celebrating, Jesse and I finally made it home in the early hours of the morning after stealing a copy of the early edition newspaper from the hotel lobby. It was the first tangible proof of Barack's win, and it felt so good to hold it in my hands!

The next morning, I awoke to the clock radio and just laid in bed, letting the events of the night before wash over me.

"We have a special celebratory song for some you today," the announcer said. *"So enjoy."* I was suddenly listening to the familiar soft melody of Will.i.am's *"Yes We Can."* It was the song that had inspired me to participate in the Obama campaign so many months ago. I felt tears sting my eyes as I sang along, having long since memorized the words.

At the office the mood was ecstatic, and still slightly disbelieving. Brian Sisolek, from Team Analytics pulled a bottle of Johnny Walker from his desk. *"I bought this bottle back in 2004 to celebrate, but obviously things didn't turn out the way we had hoped,"* he said to a group of us. *"I've had this on my desk ever since, and now I can finally open it."* We toasted the campaign in paper cups.

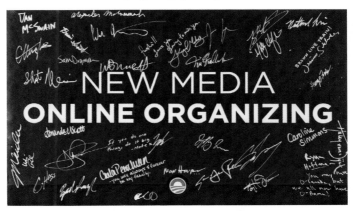

MY FAVORITE SOUVENIR FROM THE CAMPAIGN

We were all waiting for Barack's phone call, his first as the President-Elect. It was the last time we would gather around the big speakers as the Obama Campaign Team. Barack came on the line and there was thunderous applause and cheers that lasted several minutes. *"All across the country, each of you ended up being a part of my life,"* he said. *"But the main thing I want to communicate to everybody that this is your victory. Now I was a pretty good candidate, not bad,"* he continued to laughs from the team. *"But the truth is my greatest talent throughout this process was to somehow be able to assemble the best political team in history and to get you guys together. And that was really my job."* Everyone was nodding and smiling, many were teary eyed. Barack went on to praise David Plouffe's *"Singular vision, his hard work, his fearlessness,"* calling him one of the best strategic minds he had ever encountered. It was the perfect ending to an indescribable couple of months.

Before too long, I found myself wrapping up my final MyBO tasks and saying goodbye to the friends that had become like family to me. There were hugs and tears and promises to stay in touch. Loading my bags in the car, I looked up at the gorgeous fall day. There wasn't a cloud in the sky and my street was littered with golden leaves - it almost felt like summer. It was beautiful and I felt like the world was different, better somehow. I felt like dancing.

Driving home to Toronto, we passed through several states that we had won, including Michigan and Indiana. I cheered every time we crossed a state line. At a rest stop, a woman pointed to the *"Yes We Can"* sign I had put up in the window and then to the Obama car magnet that was on her own vehicle.

"Yes We Did!" She said proudly.

I couldn't agree more.

THE COUNTDOWN CLOCK IN NEW MEDIA

14 *The New Face of Government*

THE DIGITAL ADMINISTRATION

AFTER A DECIDEDLY INNOVATIVE AND CREATIVE campaign, the world watched as Barack Obama soundly defeated John McCain to become the next president of the United States. There was a collective pause as we savored the triumphant victory of a grassroots movement driven by the efforts of regular Americans. Expectations, emotions, and hopes were all running high, and all eyes were on the man who had come to symbolize an uplifting sense of possibility.

From the moment he became the president-elect, Obama ensured that his administration would continue to collaborate with the online community that had been so instrumental in his election. BarackObama.com and MyBO would become a group called Organizing for America. In addition to updating the official White House website with a sleek design, the new media team would create online websites for Obama's transition into office and his inauguration. In every online forum, Obama demonstrated his willingness to engage the American people in a more interactive democratic process.

This chapter will examine some of the initiatives launched after the election, including:

CHANGE.GOV — The transition's official website featured a crowd-sourced citizen briefing book that allowed users to submit their suggestions about important issues to Obama.

ORGANIZING FOR AMERICA — Obama hopes to turn the MyBO community into a powerful grassroots base that can help him promote his legislative agenda.

THE INAUGURATION OFFICIAL WEBSITE — Obama's inauguration marked one of the biggest social media events to date, with millions of people using social networks, blogs, and microblogs to share their experiences.

WHITEHOUSE.GOV — Obama became the first president to have a blog and a YouTube channel.

Change.gov

After briefly savoring their victory on November 4, 2008, the new media team went right back to work launching Change.gov, Obama's official transition website.

The website was designed to engage the online community in the months before Obama's inauguration and to maintain the momentum that had been built during

the course of the election. Change.gov featured a blog and pages listing job opportunities. Supporters were encouraged to submit their vision for America. In December 2008, the transition team announced that they would post all policy documents from meetings with outside organizations in order to give the public a chance to review and comment, reinforcing Obama's commitment to providing a transparent transition experience.

THE CITIZEN'S BRIEFING BOOK

In January 2009, the campaign unveiled a new way for Americans to get involved in the political process: The Citizen's Briefing Book. The

initiative invited supporters to pitch their ideas and recommendations on specific issues to the new administration. In addition to posting their own ideas, users had the ability to

vote and comment on suggestions submitted by others. Some of the most popular policy ideas included legalizing online gambling, decriminalizing the use of marijuana, and prioritizing green initiatives. The best-rated ideas were compiled into a book format and presented to the president after the inauguration on January 20, 2009.

44,000 IDEAS AND RECOMMENDATIONS WERE SUBMITTED

500,000 PEOPLE VOTED ON ONE OR MORE SUBMISSIONS

1.4 MILLION TOTAL VOTES WERE CAST

The transition team posted YouTube videos in response to the issues being raised by supporters. For example, Nancy Sutley, chair-designee for the White House Council on Environmental Quality, shared her thoughts about reducing carbon footprinting and creating green jobs. She answered specific questions that had been submitted by the online community, reinforcing the philosophy that online organizing can equal offline action.

The Obama team made the decision to license all content and user contributions on Change.gov under the Creative Commons license, which would allow anyone to use material from the site without violating any copyright laws.

JOIN THE DISCUSSION

In addition to the briefing book, the transition team hosted an ongoing discussion forum where members of Obama's policy teams shared updates and solicited feedback about particular issues. For example, Paul Schmitz, a member of the innovation and civil society team, asked the online community for help in generating the best solutions to tackle the issues of education, energy, poverty, and the environment. *"We hope that you'll let us know the social causes and service organizations that you've been part of that make a difference in your community,"* he asked supporters in an introductory video. *"We hope you'll join the discussion."*

Organizing for America

Many volunteers did not want their involvement in the campaign to end. Discussions on MyBO abounded as to how they could continue to support Obama now that he was in office. *"We are ready to roll up our sleeves and get this country back on track,"* stated one user in the Obama blog comments section. *"What's next?"* It wasn't uncommon for supporters to stop by local volunteer offices to see if there was anything that still needed to be done. The energy to bring about change was still running strong and the community looked to Obama to provide the next step. The president-elect would not disappoint.

Obama announced that the campaign's online infrastructure will be used to form a new group called Organizing for America (OFA), which will continue to uphold Obama's mission of grassroots advocacy. Organizing for America will be housed within the Democratic National Committee and will help to mobilize supporters to promote the president's agenda. The formation of this group ensured that Obama's massive email list would remain within the control of loyal supporters. The Democratic National Party now faces a learning curve as it searches for the right balance of communications, to avoid spamming subscribers and reducing the effectiveness of the messaging. The long-term impact of having such an email list remains to be seen.

OFA has introduced several initiatives aimed at increasing community activism. One example is the Pledge Project, where volunteers are asked to publicly declare their support for Obama's policies by committing to outreach activities such as canvassing or talking to their neighbors about Obama's new economy recovery plan. MyBO and Neighbor to Neighbor have been adapted for this purpose, and supporters can now join calling campaigns across the country to promote Obama's policies.

The Inauguration:
Change Has Come to America

By the time January 20, 2009, rolled around, the world was ready to see Barack Obama officially sworn in as the forty-fourth president of the United States of America. Social media played a big part in the festivities, with live streaming video feeds and extensive coverage on blogs, social networks, and microblogging sites such as Twitter. According to the Associated Press, over 7.7 million people watched online video streams of the event.

The campaign launched it's own official inauguration blog that included information about the big day, real-time updates from staff, and the opportunity for U.S. citizens to submit their inauguration photos to be included in the Official Inauguration Book.

Around the web, the inauguration dominated the conversation. 14,282 pictures were uploaded to Flickr's official Inauguration 2009 group. Facebook, in partnership with CNN, allowed users to update their Facebook status while watching the inauguration on CNN.com. The Mashable blog reported 600,000 status updates were posted through the CNN/Facebook feed. Facebook users could also send a virtual glass of champagne to friends.

FACTS (VIA MASHABLE)

- 4,000 status updates per minute were posted during the inauguration

- 8,500 status updates were recorded during the first minute of Obama's speech

- CNN reported 136 million page views

- CNN streamed to 1.3 million people simultaneously at its peak

Twitter's official blog reported a spike in traffic, up to four times the usual rate for tweets sent per minute, surpassing the traffic experienced on election night. During the president's speech, over 35,000 tweets per hour were posted containing the world "Obama."

CAN WE BE FRIENDS?

Sorryeverybody.com was launched after George Bush's reelection in 2004. Americans from across the country uploaded a photo holding up a sign apologizing for Bush's second victory.

ApologiesAccepted.com, launched in response to sorryeverybody. com featured people from around the world sending messages of hope to Americans who were demoralized by Bush's reelection. "We, wanderers of the world outside the U.S., have been touched by the initiative of www.sorryeverybody.com, and the huge amount of photos they received. The initiators of this website would like to show to the American people that they appreciated that message." – *ApologiesAccepted.com, 2004*

Helloeverybody.com "Some of us—apparently, most of us—would like to say hi to you, world. We had a rough patch there. We would have called earlier, but things were a little weird between you and us, and I wasn't sure what else there was to say. You know how it is: you think of calling, you stare at the phone, and then one day the sun is shining and you elect a black guy who reads a lot and did great in college. So, hello, world. Let's get to know each other again. We cool?" —*Helloeverybody.com, formerly Sorryeverybody.com, 2008*

Whitehouse.gov

On January 21, 2009, Obama's new media team officially claimed ownership of Whitehouse.gov, a U.S. government's official website, and unveiled the new face of the Obama Administration. For the first time, Obama's new media team had to deal with the bureaucracy of government. Staffers now had to contend with filtered web browser results and restrictive security policies that prohibited the use of instant messaging and access to social networking sites like Facebook and Twitter. President Obama faced his own challenges, as he fought to keep his BlackBerry in the face of security concerns. Luckily, he succeeded and became the first president to own a smartphone. The president has said that his daughters are among the handful of people who have his email address so that they can reach him at any time no matter where he is.

Whitehouse.gov launched to mixed reviews. The official White House blog, while the first of its kind, was criticized for not allowing readers to post comments. In addition, the author of the post isn't clearly identified, giving the blog an overall impersonal feel. *"Whitehouse.gov is just the beginning of the new administration's efforts to expand and deepen this online engagement,"* said Macon Phillips, the White House's Director of New Media, whose position has recently been elevated to "special assistant to the president," reflecting the increased importance that technology will play in Obama's government.

Obama is finding himself cut off from the very tools he used to rally supporters and build a movement. For example, the White House does not have the technology needed to send out mass e-mails or text messaging campaigns to update supporters on recent activities. There are also legal regulations that involve the collection of cell phone numbers to protect the privacy of citizens. *"This is uncharted territory,"* said Phillips in a *Washington Post* interview, acknowledging the high expectations of a tech-savvy community who has grown accustomed to sharing a certain level of accessibility with Obama.

There have been some growing pains. When the new media team posted the details of the $787 billion stimulus package online, they asked supporters to limit their feedback to 500 characters, which angered many users.

Phillips urged patience as the team adjusted to the new circumstances and within thirty-six hours the character limit was increased to 5,000. *"We're not running a campaign anymore,"* Phillips said. *"The new programs that we will roll out are more than just URLs. They are new ways to engage with citizens."*

Despite the challenges, Phillips and his team are pioneering a new era of political engagement. Obama is the first president to have a YouTube channel. His weekly video addresses are forging a new relationship with an entire generation of voters—a digitized version of Franklin D. Roosevelt's famous Fireside Chats.

SECRETARY OF STATE CLINTON: E-DIPLOMACY

Secretary of State Hillary Clinton has also embraced the Obama Administration's appreciation for new media to rebuild America's image and reputation within the global community. Clinton continuously updates her status on Facebook, Twitter, Flickr, and YouTube. Users can stay informed on Secretary Clinton's whereabouts by following her travels on an interactive map. In a new initiative, supporters can use their mobile phones to "text the secretary" their questions about the State Department, foreign policy, or anything else they have on their minds. Upon her return from a trip to the Middle East, she had received over 2,000 text messages.

Local bloggers were invited to join Clinton on her first two foreign trips, and were embedded with the traditional press corps. These initiatives are only beginning to scratch the surface of the possibilities of interacting and engaging with government.

ONLINE TOWN HALL MEETING

In March 2009, President Obama upheld his promise to open up the White House to the American people by hosting the first online town hall meeting, in a session dedicated to addressing Americans' concerns about their economy, health care, education, and the environment. Questions were asked in either written or video form and users could vote on questions submitted by others. Over 3.5 million votes were cast for questions that spanned topics ranging from unemployment to homeownership. According to the White House website, 92,937 people submitted 103,981 questions and cast 3,602,695 votes.

There was one issue that continues to be popular much to the president's dismay. *"I have to say that there was one question that was voted on that ranked fairly high, and that was whether legalizing marijuana would improve the economy and job creation. I don't know what this says about the online audience,"* he joked.

For new media, adjusting to the structure of being a government institution after running a quick and agile campaign is an ongoing process. Government has less maneuvering room and a much smaller margin for error. And yet they continue to pursue initiatives designed to unite the American people around the issues that matter to them. They have awakened a new age of digital activism and political involvement. These exciting events are continuing to unfold at the time of this writing.

While the full potential of mobilizing an online community to impact a legislative agenda remains to be seen, increasingly sophisticated tools will no doubt yield a new generation of savvy users who are ready to engage with political leaders. No one is sure if these developments will revolutionize democracy or unleash a fickle audience that can turn against its creator. As communication with supporters and consumers through social media tools becomes a normal part of integrated digital strategy, the next site or application may yet turn everything we think we know on its head. Who knows what new developments will guide the next election, and what each side will innovate in order to survive the next round.

The Obama campaign was unlike any other in history. Many people were changed during this campaign, and I count myself as one of them. From having the opportunity to work with Joe Rospars and Chris Hughes as they designed the most powerful online grassroots community to speaking with other volunteers who were help-ing Obama in their own small way, I was uplifted by their spirit and determination. More importantly, for the first time in a long time, I feel hopeful that we the people can change the existing political systems and elect leaders who are accountable, honest, and transparent.

Index

Numbers

E

Edwards, John, votes received in Iowa, 23

"Eight in '08" series, 131

Election Day
    call from Fox News, 168
    Obama's acceptance speech, 171
    win in Ohio, 168

email communication, tone of, 112

email list, growing, 100

email program, management of, 113–114

email team
    escalating involvement strategy of, 102–103
    mandate of, 101
    mobilization of, 102–103

emails. *See also* campaign emails
    advantage of, 100
    defining purpose of, 112
    Elections Matter (Gore), 102
    Last Minute Attacks (Plouffe), 103–104
    power of, 105
    receiving from campaign, 100–101

end user, thinking like, 156–157, 161

Environmentalists for Obama, 82

escalating involvement strategy, 102–103

events, organization of, 84–85

F

Facebook ads, money spent on, 157

Facebook groups, Students for Obama, 7–8

Facebook social network, strategy employed with, 139–140

FaithBase profile, 138

February 5, 2008 (Super Tuesday), 28

fellows, commitment of, 41

fellowship, creation of, 40

Fey, Tina, 18

Fifty-State Strategy, 47, 50

Fightthesmears.com, 41

FISA (Foreign Intelligence Surveillance Act), amendment to, 80–83

Five Calls campaign, 33–34

Florida Women for Obama Campaign for Change, 82

"the fold," headlines above, 68–69

food, sharing, 61–62

Frere-Jones, Tobias, 68

Front Row to History email (Obama), 108–109

Ft. Collins, Colorado, Dan of, 85

Fullerton, Tim, 113–114

funding, source of, 11

fundraising
    on MyBO, 77–78
    online, 51
    strategy toward, 51

fundraising campaign of March 2007, 9–10

fundraising dinner, new model for, 11

fundraising status, online update of, 25–26

fundraising strategy, use of "non-tests," 108

G

Gage, Alexander, 47–49

gaming ad network, use of, 157

Geer, Stephen
    emails drafted by, 100
    mobilization efforts of, 102–103
    "non-tests," 108
    power of email, 105–106
    testing email, 109–111

Generation Obama, 85

Get Out the Vote campaign, 33–34

get out the vote campaigns, participation in, 95

Get Out the Vote (GOTV) initiatives, 41

GLEE online community, 138

goal-specific campaigns, participation in, 93

Golden, Wendy H., 36

O

Obama, Barack
  as agent of change, 22
  audience for, 12
  call to Angela Berg, 10–11
  versus Clinton, Hillary, 18,
    20–21
  conference calls with, 56, 62
  last call to headquarters, 173
  Message from the debate email,
    107
  message on HQ Blog, 90
  nomination of, 37
  participation in Yahoo Answers,
    13
  strengths of, 13
  text message from, 119
  total funds raised by, 51
  victory in Iowa, 23
  victory in North Carolina, 37
  victory in Oregon, 37
  victory in Texas caucus, 34
  victory in Vermont primary, 34
  victories in Wyoming and
    Mississippi, 34
Obama blog. See blog network
Obama Bot, 55–56
Obama emails, content of, 102
"The Obama Family Cookbook," 86
Obama Fellowship Program, 40
Obama headquarters, arrival at, 54.
  See also HQ blog
Obama Mobile, launch of, 120
Obama NYC, 85
Obama "O" logo, design of, 66
Obama rallies, impact on emails,
  100
Obama Supporter Rapid Response
  Team, 21
Obama Works venture, 84
Obama YouTube channel, link on
  iPhone, 122
Obama's administration, pitching
  ideas to, 177–178
Obama's emails
  community organizing, 42
  republication on blog, 131

Obama's policies, declaring support
  for, 179
Obama's positions, information on
  iPhones, 123
OFA (Organizing for America),
  176, 179
offensive comments, response to,
  130
offline activities, emphasizing in
  MyBO, 79
offline events, organization of,
  84–85
offline participation, laying
  groundwork for, 19
Ohio
  Clinton's victory in, 34
  contacting voters in, 33
  primary in, 32
  winning on Election Day, 168
  working-class population in, 32
online advertising
  cost of, 156
  on social networks, 157
online audience, addressing, 27
online communities
  building, 88
  feeling pulse of, 129
  growth of, 6–8
  maturity by August 2008, 43
  mobilizing, 95
  rewarding actions in, 88
  spirit of, 84
  storytelling aspect of, 11
online donations. See also donors
  amounts raised from, 108
  personalizing of, 10
online fundraising, 51
online grassroots movement,
  building of, 48
online notes, writing, 10, 22–24
online organizing
  2004 Howard Dean campaign,
    46–48
  Hoffman, Ryan internship,
    97–98
  ánd offline action, 19–20, 23, 48
online phonebanking tool, use of,
  32–34

COLOPHON

This book was typeset in Mercury Display & Text,
Headlines are set in Chronicle Display and Knockout, all
original designs of Hoefler & Frere-Jones, of New York.
Their website is www.typography.com

The book was digitally-crafted in Adobe® InDesign CS3.

The text pages are printed on 60# Influence Matte.